Beaded Cross-Stitch Treasures

Designs from Mill Hill

Gay Bowles

Sterling Publishing Co., Inc. New York

A Sterling/Chapelle Book

Dedication

This book of needlework art is dedicated to
Jill Siegler, Vice President of Mill Hill Design. Jill's creative
spirit, close friendship, and constant support have been a
beacon throughout the Mill Hill years.

Special thanks to our Mill Hill Design staff whose
collaborative effort made this project possible, Ellen
Scheidler, Mary Jurgens-Jones, and Gina Dedolph.

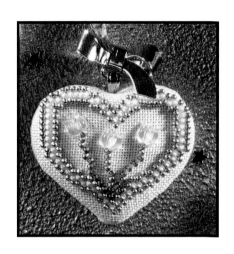

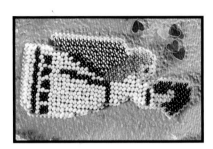

Chapelle Ltd.

Owner
Jo Packham

Editor
Karmen Quinney

Staff

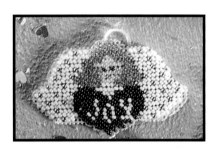

Marie Barber, Ann Bear, Areta Bingham, Kass Burchett, Rebecca Christensen, Brenda Doncouse,
Dana Durney, Marilyn Goff, Holly Hollingsworth, Susan Jorgensen, Barbara Milburn, Linda Orton,
Leslie Ridenour, Cindy Stoeckl, Gina Swapp

Library of Congress Cataloging-in-Publication Data

Bowles, Gay.
    Beaded cross-stitch treasures: designs from Mill Hill / Gay
Bowles.
      p.   cm.
    Includes index.
    "A Sterling/Chapelle Book"
    ISBN 0-8069-5527-9
    1. Cross-stitch   2. Beadwork Patterns.   I. Title.
TT778.C76B69   1999   99-35626
746.44'304—dc21   CIP

10 9 8 7 6 5 4

A Sterling/Chapelle Book

First paperback edition published in 2000 by
Sterling Publishing Company, Inc.
387 Park Avenue South, New York, N.Y. 10016
Produced by Chapelle Ltd.
P.O. Box 9252, Newgate Station, Ogden, Utah 84409
© 1999 by Chapelle Limited
Distributed in Canada by Sterling Publishing
℅ Canadian Manda Group, One Atlantic Avenue, Suite 105
Toronto, Ontario, Canada M6K 3E7
Distributed in Great Britain by Chrysalis Books
64 Brewery Road, London N7 9NT, England
Distributed in Australia by Capricorn Link (Australia) Pty. Ltd.
P.O. Box 704, Windsor, NSW 2756 Australia

Printed in China
All rights reserved

Sterling ISBN 0-8069-5527-9 Trade
            0-8069-5545-7 Paper

Needlework supplies for the projects in this book may be
purchased at your local retail needlework store. To locate a
store near you, please call (608) 754-9466; write
P. O. Box 1060, Janesville, WI 53547-1060; or visit our web
site at www.millhill.com.

If you have any questions or comments, please contact:
Chapelle Ltd., Inc., P. O. Box 9252 Ogden, UT 84409
(801) 621-2777 • FAX (801) 621-2788 • E-mail Chapelle1
@ aol.com

The written instructions, photographs, designs, patterns,
and projects in this volume are intended for the personal
use of the reader and may be reproduced for that purpose
only. Any other use, especially commercial use, is forbidden
under law without the written permission of the copyright
holder. Every effort has been made to ensure that all of the
information in this book is accurate.

Due to differing conditions, tools, and individual skills, the
publisher cannot be responsible for any injuries, losses,
and/or other damages which may result from the use of the
information in this book.

Contents

With each attached bead and treasure, I give you a piece of my heart.

Information to Know

• Read Special Instructions and Notes by individual graphs before starting to stitch.

• Notice that graphs do not overlap.

• Keep in mind that these are authentic Mill Hill Glass Beads. The sizes of the beads are not exactly uniform. This will not matter in the finished piece and actually makes for very interesting stitching.

• Try running the thread back through the line of beads after you have finished stitching the row, in order to keep a row of beads straight that may seem a little crooked.

• Attach glass treasures with designated floss and beads after entire project has been stitched and beaded.

Abbreviations to Know

Abbreviations are used in the codes throughout the book. Following are the abbreviations and their meanings:

ATT W/FLOSS = attach with floss

ATT W/BEAD/FLOSS = attach with bead and floss

UWT = used with treasure

UWB = used with bead

*see note = refer to information following Note:

Stitch Count: = width x height

Cross-stitch Items to Know

Fabric for Cross-stitch

Counted cross-stitch is worked on even-weave fabrics. These fabrics are manufactured speci-fically for counted-thread embroidery, and are woven with the same number of vertical as horizontal threads per inch.

Because the number of threads in the fabric is equal in each direction, each stitch will be the same size. The number of threads per inch in even-weave fabrics determines the size of a finished design.

Number of Strands

The number of strands used per stitch varies, depending on the fabric used. Generally, the rule to follow for cross-stitching is three strands on Aida 11, two strands on Aida 14, one or two strands on Aida 18 (depending on desired thickness of stitches), and one strand on Hardanger 22.

For backstitching, use one strand on all fabrics. When completing a French Knot (FK), use two strands and one wrap on all fabrics, unless otherwise directed.

Finished Design Size

To determine the size of the finished design, divide the stitch count by the number of threads per inch of fabric. When design is stitched over two threads, divide stitch count by half the threads per inch. For example, if a design with a stitch count of 120 width and 250 height was stitched on a 28 count linen over two threads making it 14 count), the finished size would be 8⅝" x 17⅞".

$$120 \div 14" = 8\tfrac{5}{8}" \text{ (width)}$$

$$250 \div 14" = 17\tfrac{7}{8}" \text{ (height)}$$

$$\text{Finished size} = 8\tfrac{5}{8}" \times 17\tfrac{7}{8}"$$

Preparing Fabric

Cut fabric at least 3" larger on all sides than the finished design size to ensure enough space for desired assembly. To prevent fraying, whip-stitch or machine-zigzag along the raw edges or apply liquid fray preventive.

Needles for Cross-stitch

Blunt needles should slip easily through the fabric holes without piercing fabric threads. For fabric with 11 or fewer threads per inch, use a tapestry needle #24; for 14 threads per inch, use a tapestry needle #24, #26, or #28; for 18 or more threads per inch, use a tapestry needle #26 or #28. Avoid leaving the needle in the design area of the fabric. It may leave rust or a permanent impression on the fabric.

Floss

All numbers and color names on the codes represent the DMC brand of floss. Use 18" lengths of floss. For best coverage, separate the strands and dampen with a wet sponge, then put together the number of strands required for the fabric used.

Centering Design on Fabric

Fold the fabric in half horizontally, then vertically. Place a pin in the intersection to mark the center. Locate the center of the design on the graph. To help in centering the larger designs, arrows are provided at left- and right-side center and top and bottom center. Begin stitching all designs at the center point of the graph and fabric.

Centering on Perforated Paper

On the wrong side of the perforated paper, using a pencil, draw diagonals from the exact corners. Where the lines cross is the exact center.

Center

Securing Floss

Insert needle up from the underside of the fabric at starting point. Hold 1" of thread behind the fabric and stitch over it, securing with the first few stitches. To finish thread, run under four or more stitches on the back of the design. Avoid knotting floss, unless working on clothing.

Another method of securing floss is the waste knot. Knot floss and insert needle down from the right top side of the fabric about 1" from design area. Work several stitches over the thread to secure. Cut off the knot later.

Carrying Floss

To carry floss, run floss under the previously worked stitches on the back. Do not carry thread across any fabric that is not or will not be stitched. Loose threads, especially dark ones, will show through the fabric.

Cleaning Finished Design

When stitching is finished, soak the fabric in cold water with a mild soap for five to ten minutes. Rinse well and roll in a towel to remove excess water. Do not wring. Place the piece face down on a dry towel and iron on a warm setting until the fabric is dry.

Stitches to Know

Alicia Lace (AL)

Worked diagonally over two threads on each row with the direction of the stitch alternating in each row. The first stitch on the second and proceeding rows may need to be compensated. Adjust stitch as necessary.

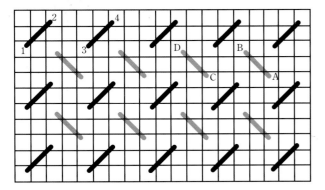

1. Insert needle up between woven threads at 1.

2. Go down at 2.

3. Come up at 3, go down at 4. Continue until length of row is filled.

4. Come up at A, go down at B.

5. Come up at C, go down at D. Continue until length of row is filled.

6. Repeat to fill design area.

Backstitch (BS)

(one strand)

1. Insert needle up between woven threads at 1.

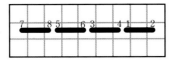

2. Go down at 2, crossing two threads to the right.

3. Come up at 3. Go down at 4, crossing two threads to the right.

4. Repeat to fill design area.

Bead Clusters

Dimension is added to counted bead embroidery by clustering the beads. On the graphs, the stitches are graphed at the angle and length desired. The amount of beads to pick up is indicated on the graph. Worked in a row, one at a time in an area.

1. Pick up several beads on a working thread and stitch as one stitch.

Bead Loops

1. At each marked symbol on the graph, pick up the amount of beads indicated.

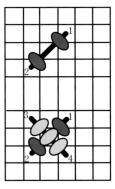

2. Insert the needle up between woven threads and through the first bead, go down in the same hole to form a loop. Adjust each loop before going on to the next one.

Bead Posie

1. Insert needle up between woven threads at 1.

2. Pick up two specified beads. Go down at 2.

3. Come up at 3, pick up three specified beads. Go down at 4.

4. Tuck middle bead into center, using tight tension to "pop" center bead in place.

Counted Bead Embroidery

Worked with a half-cross stitch. All stitches must go in the same direction in order for the beads to lay properly. Do not jump more than three or four stitches without first securing the thread on the back.

1. Begin in lower left corner. Insert needle up between woven threads at 1. Pick up specified bead. Go down at 2 to attach bead and finish stitch.

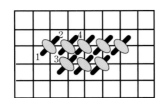

Cross-stitch (XS)

(two strands)

Worked in a row, one at a time in an area.

1. Insert needle up between woven threads at 1.

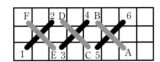

2. Go down at 2, forming a diagonal stitch.

3. Come up at 3 and down at 4, etc.

4. To complete the top stitches creating an "x", come up at A, go down at B. Come up at C, go down at D, etc. All top stitches should lie in the same direction.

Detached Chain Stitch (DC)

(two strands)

1. Insert needle up between woven threads at 1.

2. Go down at 2, using same opening as 1.

3. Come up at 3, crossing under two threads. Pull through, holding floss under needle to form loop.

4. Go down at 4, crossing one thread.

Diagonal Satin Stitch (DS)

(two strands)

1. Insert needle up between woven threads at 1.

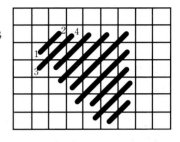

2. Go down at 2, crossing one thread, forming a diagonal stitch.

3. Come up at 3, go down at 4, forming another smooth diagonal stitch that is slightly longer than the first.

4. Repeat to fill design area.

Eyelet Stitch (ES)

(two strands)

1. Insert needle up between woven threads at 1.

2. Go down at 2 (center). Continue around center 8 times, bringing needle down through center each time.

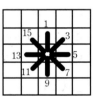

Faggot Stitch (FS)

(two strands)

Worked in a stair-step manner down the fabric then back up the fabric.

1. Insert needle up between woven threads at 1.

2. Go down at 2.

3. Traveling diagonally across the back of fabric, come up at 3, go down at 4.

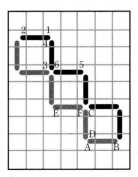

4. Traveling diagonally across the back of the fabric, come up at 5, go down at 6, etc.

5. Repeat the same stair-step motion (A–F) working up the other side of the stitches in the same manner.

Fluffy French Knot (FFK)

(four strands)

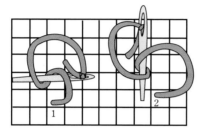

1. Insert needle up between woven threads at 1.

2. Loosely wrap floss around needle four times.

3. Go down at 2, crossing one thread next to 1. Pull floss tight as needle is pushed down through fabric.

4. Carry floss across back of work between knots.

Four-sided Stitch (FSS)

(two strands)

Worked using normal tension, or using pulled tension for a lacy effect.

1. Insert needle up between woven threads at 1.

2. Go down at 2.

3. Traveling diagonally across the back of the fabric, come up at 3, go down at 4.

4. Traveling diagonally across the back of the fabric come up at 5, go down at 6.

5. Traveling diagonally across the back of the fabric come up at 7, go down at 8.

6. Repeat as needed after the initial four sides of the first stitch are complete, the following stitches that lie side by side need only have three sides. Stitch 7–8 is a shared stitch with the next four-sided stitch.

French Knot (FK)

(one strand)

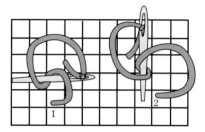

1. Insert needle up between woven threads at 1.

2. Loosely wrap floss once around needle.

3. Go down at 2, crossing one thread next to 1. Pull floss tight as needle is pushed down through fabric.

4. Carry floss across back of work between knots.

Half-cross Stitch (HX)

(two strands)

Worked in a row horizontally from left to right.

1. Insert needle up between woven threads at 1.

2. Go down at 2, forming a diagonal stitch.

3. Come up at 3 and down at 4, etc.

4. Repeat to fill design area.

Herringbone Stitch (HB)

(two strands)

Worked with diagonal and horizontal stitches.

1. Insert needle up between woven threads at 1.

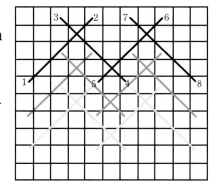

2. Go down at 2. Traveling horizontally across the back, come up at 3, go down at 4, making an "X".

3. Come up at 5, go down at 6. Come up at 7, go down at 8, etc.

4. Repeat to fill design area.

Kloster Block (KB)

(one strand)

Worked by stitching five vertical or horizontal satin stitches over four threads. When turning a corner, a hole is shared. Do not carry a thread diagonally when turning a corner. To begin and end, go under two blocks, take a backstitch in the center of the third block and continue under two more blocks. This will ensure the thread will not come lose.

When working a kloster block around a project, check frequently to make certain the kloster blocks on the opposite sides are stitched in the same direction and over the same threads.

1. Insert needle up between woven threads at 1.

2. Go down at 2.

3. Come up at 3, go down at 4.

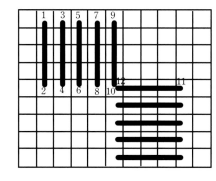

4. Come up at 5, go down at 6, etc.

5. Repeat to fill design area.

Large Cross-stitch (LXS)

(one strand)

1. Insert needle up between woven threads at 1.

2. Go down at 2, forming a diagonal stitch.

3. Come up at 3, go down at 4, etc.

4. Repeat to fill design area.

Long Stitch (LS)

(two strands)

1. Insert needle up between woven threads at 1.

2. Go down at 2, crossing two threads. Pull flat. Repeat 1–2 for each stitch. Stitch may be horizontal, vertical, or diagonal.

3. Repeat to fill design area.

Mosaic Stitch (MS)

(six strands)

1. Insert needle up between woven threads at 1.

2. Go down at 2.

3. Come up at 3, go down at 4.

4. Come up at 5, go down at 6.

5. Repeat to fill design area.

Satin Stitch (SS)

(two strands)

1. Insert needle up between woven threads at 1.

2. Go down at 2, forming a straight stitch.

3. Come up at 3, go down at 4, forming another smooth straight stitch that is slightly longer than the first.

4. Repeat to fill design area.

Smyrna Cross-stitch (SX)

(two strands)

1. Make a Cross-stitch (XS) as the base of this stitch.

2. Place a vertical stitch on top of the cross-stitch. Come up at 5, go down at 6.

3. Come up at 7, go down at 8, with a horizontal stitch centered on top of the vertical stitch.

Uneven Cross-stitch

(two strands)

1. Insert needle up between woven threads at 1.

2. Go down at 2.

3. Come up at 3, go down at 4.

4. Come up at 5, go down at 6.

5. Come up at 7, go down at 8, etc.

6. Repeat to fill design area.

Beading

• Separate floss into single strands.

• Hold back the beginning thread (two strands of floss in designated color) until it is covered with stitches. Or begin with a waste knot on the front side. Cover this thread on the back with stitches as you work.

• Make certain all other "starting" or "stopping" threads are woven securely under worked threads on the back. Note: If you have difficulty putting two strands of floss into the eye of the needle, put one strand through the eye and pull the end down to meet other end so there are two working strands.

Beading Fabric

Glass seed beads, frosted glass beads, and antique glass beads should be stitched on fabrics with a stitch count of approximately 14 per inch. Crowding may result on higher count fabrics. For higher count fabrics, use petite glass beads.

Beading Needles

Needle sizes #9 applique quilting needle or #10 beading needle are recommended for seed beads and treasures. Use #10 beading needle when working with petite beads. Use a #24, #26, and #28 tapestry needle for stitching on linen or Aida.

Beading Sizes

Beading sizes of Mill Hill beads correspond to prestrung seed beads. Glass seed beads, frosted glass beads, and antique glass beads are #11. Petite glass beads are #14. Bugle beads come in small (5 mm), medium (10 mm), and large (15 mm).

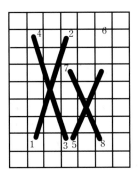

Center Hole Treasures

Center hole treasures may be attached with a seed bead. Using a single strand of floss, come up through the hole in the treasure. Pick up a bead and return the needle through the hole in the treasure.

They may be attached with floss only. Using a single strand of floss, go over the top of the treasure, setting the floss into a ridge of glass so the floss is nearly invisible. This is useful with hearts and small flowers. When using this method for attaching small flowers, go over the flower for each petal—this adds additional interest to the treasure.

Center hole treasures may also be attached with a French Knot (FK). Using two strands of floss, come up through the hole in the treasure. Make a French Knot (FK) and return the needle through the hole in the treasure.

Channel Hole Treasures

Channel hole treasures may be attached with floss. Using one strand of floss, go through the channel hole twice to secure.

The projects in this book can be finished in a variety of ways. The porcelain and crystal boxes are elegant and easy ways to finish small pieces. They work up quickly and have a fabulous finished look.

Try stitching one of the small pins that are shown on perforated paper on Aida or linen. Finish it in a porcelain or crystal box. The lids come ready to finish—just add fabric and stitching. The look will be changed completely from the perforated pin featured in the book.

The projects shown as perforated pins or ornaments are also cute framed in small frames. Use strip magnets on the back to make refrigerator magnets.

Pins

The heart charms on page 30 are shown finished as pins, but they can be made into Christmas ornaments, necklaces, framed, or stitched on a premade pillow or a band.

The projects shown on stitched bands can be applied to premade pillow tops, used as banners on wreaths, or as basket or candle bands. Stitch a border from one of the samplers on narrow banding and use as a bookmark.

Band

THE COLORS OF BEADS AND FLOSS ARE SIMPLY SUGGESTIONS. THE STITCHING POSSIBILITIES ARE ENDLESS. REMEMBER THE USES FOR THESE PROJECTS ARE AS VARIED AS YOU CHOOSE—THERE ARE NO LIMITS TO CREATIVITY.

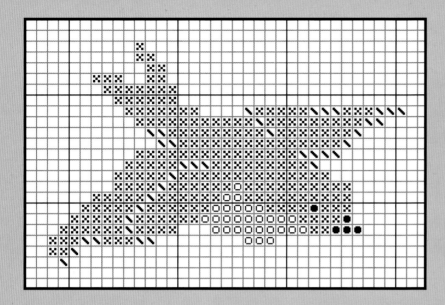

Blue Bird

Stitch Count: 33 x 21

Fabric: Perforated paper, 14 count, white

Mill Hill Beads			
	SYMBOL	**ATT W/FLOSS**	**#PKGS**
2006	✖	White	1
2003	○	White	1
358	╲	White	1
2014	●	White	1

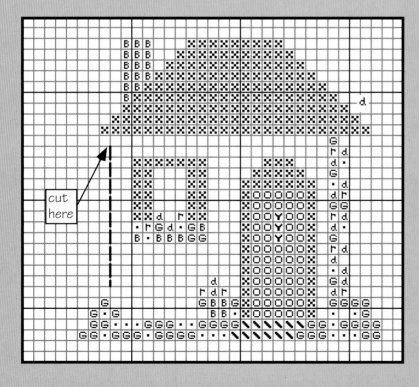

Cottage

Stitch Count: 28 x 28

Fabric: Perforated paper, 14 count, white

Mill Hill Beads			
	SYMBOL	**ATT W/FLOSS**	**#PKGS**
2015	✖	White	1
167	G	White	1
556	○	White	1
150	╲	White	1
553	⌐	White	1
221	B	White	1
148	Y	White	1
2005	d	White	1
332	·	White	1

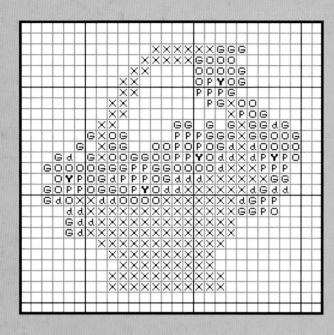

Spring Basket

Stitch Count: 24 x 23

Fabric: Perforated paper, 14 count, cream

Mill Hill Beads			
	SYMBOL	ATT W/FLOSS	#PKGS
556	✕	Ecru	1
553	P	Ecru	1
2005	o	Ecru	1
561	G	Ecru	1
332	d	Ecru	1
2002	Y	Ecru	1

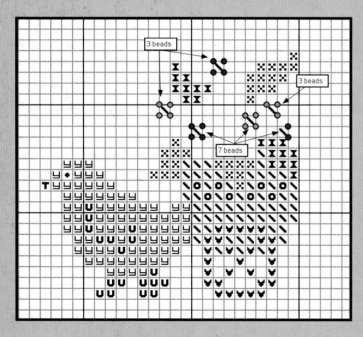

Chick Cart

Stitch Count: 24 x 23

Fabric: Perforated paper, 14 count, white

Mill Hill Beads			
	SYMBOL	ATT W/FLOSS	#PKGS
275	T	White	1
332	I	White	1
2019	u	White	1
479	✿	White	1
358	●	White	1
2004	＼	White	1
221	♥	White	1
2002	५	White	1
167	✕	White	1
2001	○	White/bead loops (5)	1
2003	●	White/bead loops (7)	1

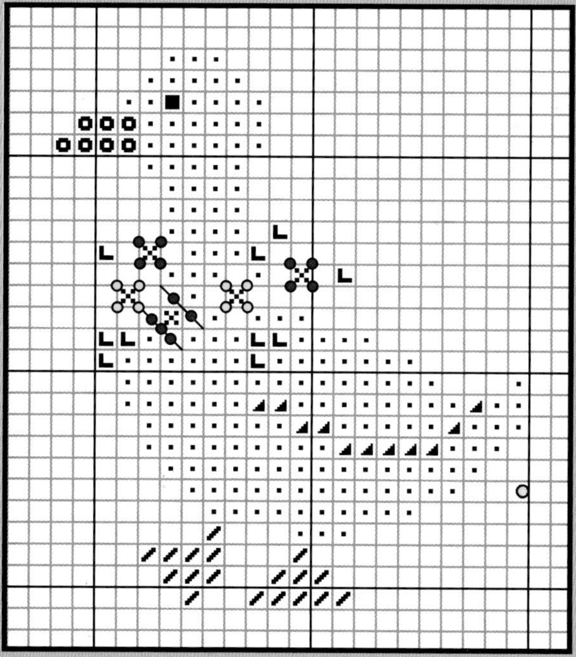

Spring Goose

Stitch Count: 22 x 26

Fabric: Perforated paper, 14 count, white

Mill Hill Beads			
	SYMBOL	ATT W/FLOSS	#PKGS
150	◢	White	1
358	■	White	1
148	●	White	1
275	/	White	1
479	·	White	1
167	L	White	1
128	⁙	White	1
2004	●	White/bead loops(4)	1
2026	○	White/bead loops/clusters(3)	1

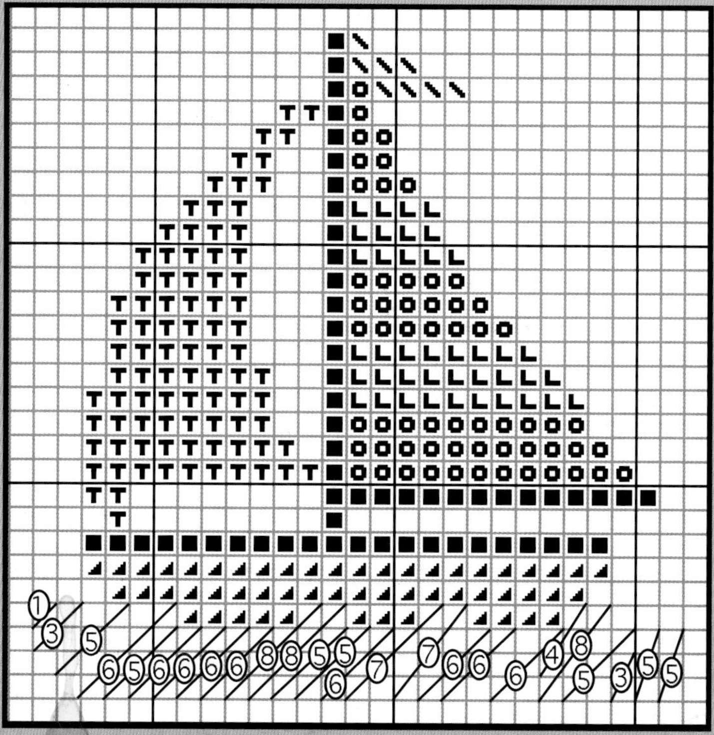

Sailboat

Stitch Count: 27 x 28

Fabric: Perforated paper, 14 count, white

Note: Number in circle indicates amount of beads to use in each cluster.

Mill Hill Beads			
	SYMBOL	ATT W/FLOSS	#PKGS
968	◢	White	1
2021	■	White	1
2022	T	White	1
479	O	White	1
20	\	White	1
2013	L	White	1
2015	*see note	White/clusters	1

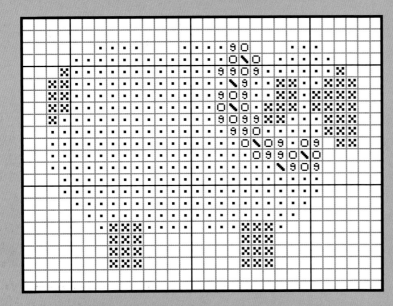

Sheep

Stitch Count: 26 x 19

Fabric: Perforated paper, 14 count, white

Mill Hill Beads			
	SYMBOL	**ATT W/FLOSS**	**#PKGS**
479	·	White	1
553	○	White	1
561	ə	White	1
81	✕	White	1
2005	❨	White	1

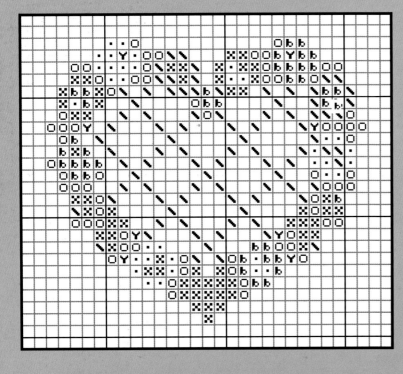

Trellis Heart

Stitch Count: 27 x 24

Fabric: Perforated paper, 14 count, white

Mill Hill Beads			
	SYMBOL	**ATT W/FLOSS**	**#PKGS**
553	✕	White	1
561	○	White	1
2005	❨	White	1
2002	Y	White	1
168	b	White	1
252	·	White	1

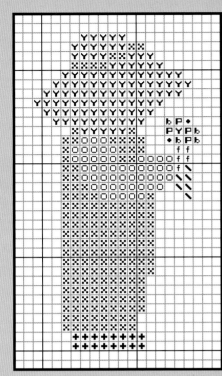

Country Boy

Stitch Count: 18 x 34

Fabric: Perforated paper, 14 count, white

Mill Hill Beads			
	SYMBOL	ATT W/FLOSS	#PKGS
2015	✖	White	1
2002	Y	White	1
275	▢	White	1
81	✦	White	1
145	f	White	1
146	♭	White	1
332	＼	White	1
252	●	White	1
2005	P	White	1

Umbrella

Stitch Count: 26 x 26

Fabric: Perforated paper, 14 count, white

Mill Hill Beads			
	SYMBOL	ATT W/FLOSS	#PKGS
358	◢	White	1
553	✿	White	1
479	–	White	1
2009	✖	White	1
2022	■	White	1
2026	·	White	1

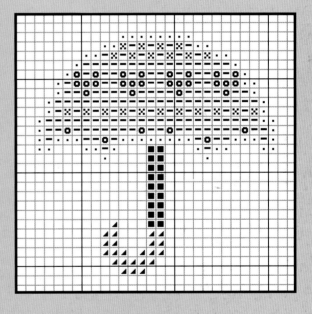

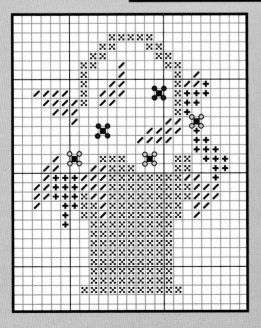

Violet Basket

Stitch Count: 21 x 28

Fabric: Perforated paper, 14 count, cream

Mill Hill Beads			
	SYMBOL	ATT W/FLOSS	#PKGS
128	■	Ecru	1
167	✦	Ecru	1
332	╱	Ecru	1
556	✖	Ecru	1
168	●	Ecru/bead loops(5)	1
252	○	Ecru/bead loops(9)	1

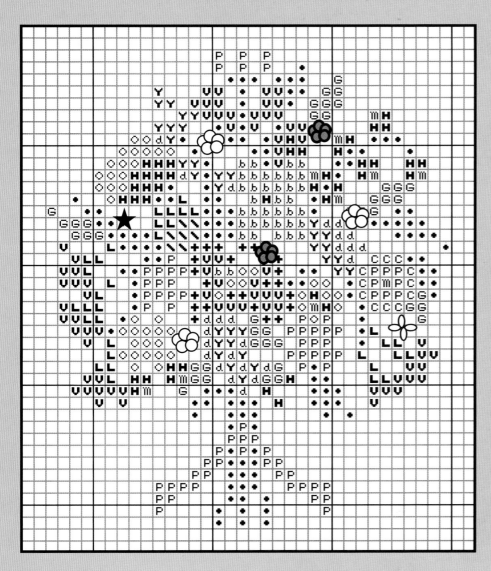

Floral Bouquet

Stitch Count: 34 x 40

Fabric: Linen, 28 count, antique ivory

DMC Floss	
	XS
224	c
315	m
340	\
503	G
727	d
778	◇
3042	+

Mill Hill Beads			
	SYMBOL	ATT W/FLOSS	#PKGS
2019	Y	727	1
2025	U	3042	1
3020	H	315	1
3051	P	224	1
40161	UWT	Ecru	1
40252	b	793	1
45270	•	503	1
60168	L	340	1

Mill Hill Treasures			
	SYMBOL	ATT W/BEAD/FLOSS	#PKGS
12210	✿	40161/Ecru	2
12149	❀	40161/Ecru	1
12150	★	40161/Ecru	1
12152	✤	40161/Ecru	1

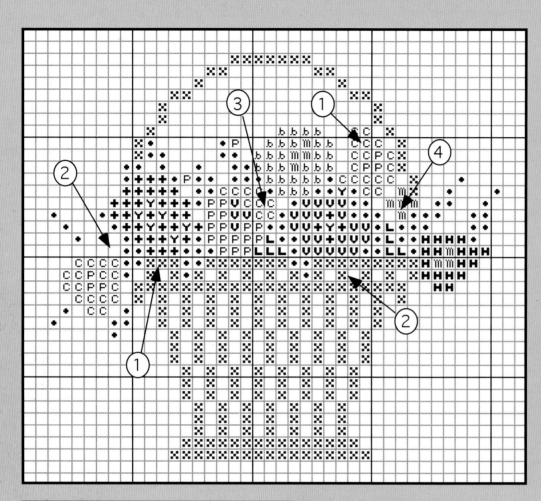

Woven Basket

Stitch Count: 38 x 34

Fabric: Linen,
28 count, antique ivory

DMC Floss	
	XS
224	c
315	ɱ
433⟩ 840	✕
3042	✛

Mill Hill Beads			
	SYMBOL	ATT W/FLOSS	#PKGS
2019	Y	727	1
2025	U	3042	1
3020	H	315	1
3051	P	224	1
40123	UWT	224	1
40252	♭	793	1
45270	•	503	1
60168	L	340	1

Mill Hill Treasures			
	SYMBOL	ATT W/BEAD/FLOSS	#PKGS
12152	①	40123/224	1
12147	②	40123/224	1
12150	③	40123/224	1
12149	④	40123/224	1

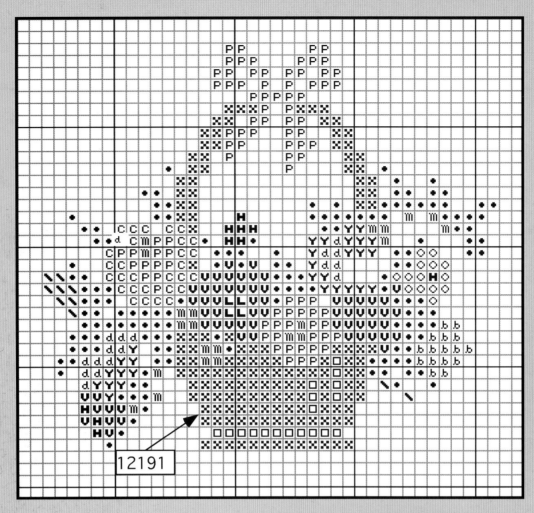

Easter Flower
Basket

Stitch Count: 38 x 34

Fabric: Linen,
28 count, ivory

Note: Refer to graph
for treasure
placement.

DMC Floss	
	XS
224	c
315	m
340	\
433	□
433〉840	⊠
727	d
778	○

Mill Hill Beads			
	SYMBOL	ATT W/FLOSS	#PKGS
2019	Y	727	1
2025	U	3042	1
3020	H	315	1
3051	P	224	1
40252	b	793	1
45270	•	503	1
60168	L	340	1

Mill Hill Treasures			
	SYMBOL	ATT W/FLOSS	#PKGS
12191	*see note	Ecru	1

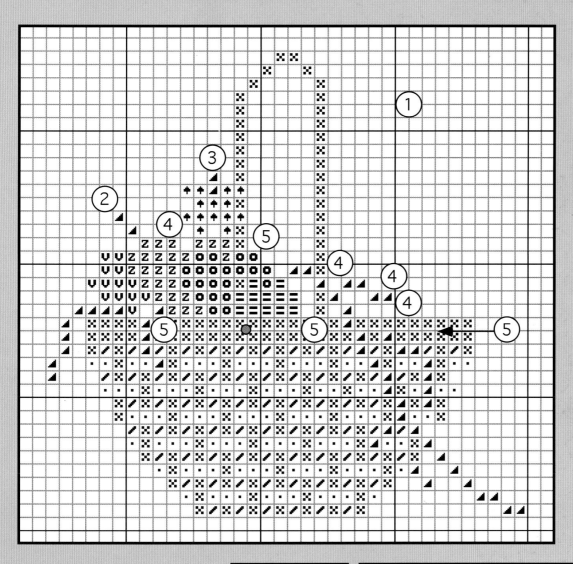

Beaded Basket

Stitch Count: 36 x 35

Fabric: Linen, 28 count, antique ivory

Special Instructions: After stitching is complete, add a bow to the front of the basket with mauve floss. Secure the bow by going over the knot with a crystal bead and ecru floss.

DMC Floss		
	XS	Bow
3727		⬤
223	+	
341	∪	
522	◢	
840	✕	
841	·	
842	╱	

Mill Hill Beads			
	SYMBOL	ATT W/FLOSS	#PKGS
123	=	Ecru	1
556	▢	Ecru	1
2012	z	Ecru	1
40161	UWT	Ecru	1

Mill Hill Treasures			
	SYMBOL	ATT W/BEAD/FLOSS	#PKGS
12121	①	/Ecru	1
12155	②	40161/Ecru	1
12153	③	40161/Ecru	1
12147	④	40161/Ecru	2
12143	⑤	40161/Ecru	2

Pastel Borders

Stitch Count: 107 x 199

Fabric: Linen, 28 count, antique white

DMC Floss	
	XS
502	✶

Mill Hill Treasures			
	SYMBOL	ATT W/BEAD/FLOSS	#PKGS
12143	🍃	40161/Ecru	3
12063	🌰	40161/Ecru	13
12013	✴	40161/Ecru	3
12210	🌸	40161/Ecru	4
12005	🌼	40161/Ecru	6
13001	◯	40161/Ecru	6
12155	🌷	40161/Ecru	15
12212	🌺	40161/Ecru	7
13021	◓	40161/Ecru	2
12075	♡	40161/Ecru	3
12064	🪶	40161/Ecru	10

Mill Hill Beads			
	SYMBOL	ATT W/FLOSS	#PKGS
123	✿	Ecru	1
148	I	Ecru	1
553	╱	Ecru	1
2005	L	Ecru	1
2006	H	Ecru	2
2018	◆	Ecru	1
2019	◇	Ecru	1
2026	✦	Ecru	1
40161	UWT	Ecru	1
62034	U	Ecru	1
62041	⊡	Ecru	1
62046	■	Ecru	1
62047	Z	Ecru	1
62048	◦	Ecru	1
65270	■	Ecru	2
70123	╱	Ecru	1
70123	▨▨▨▨	Ecru	1
72005	◇◇◇◇	Ecru	1

Top left

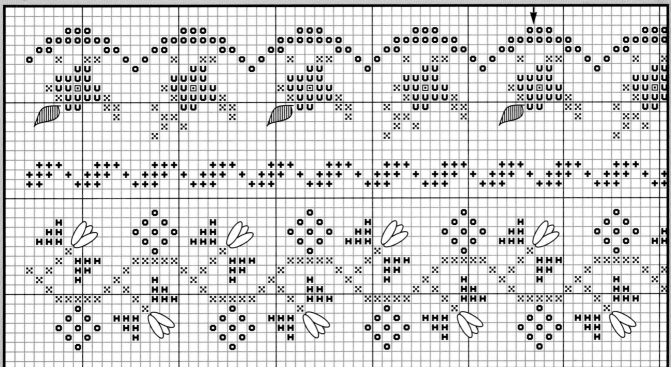

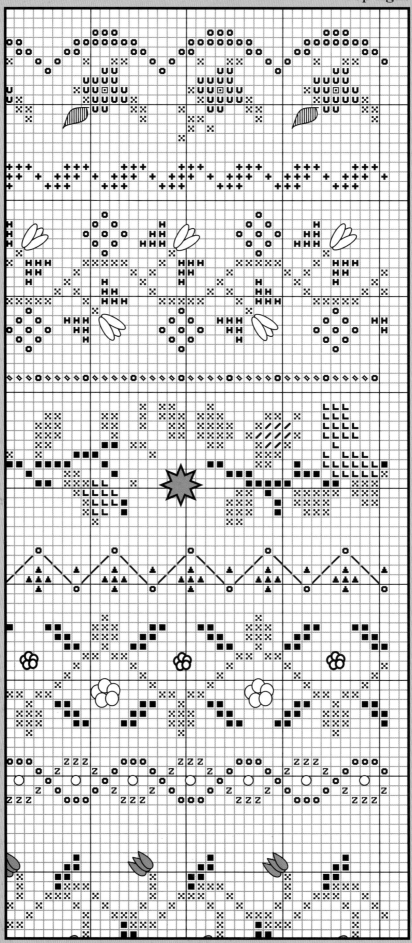

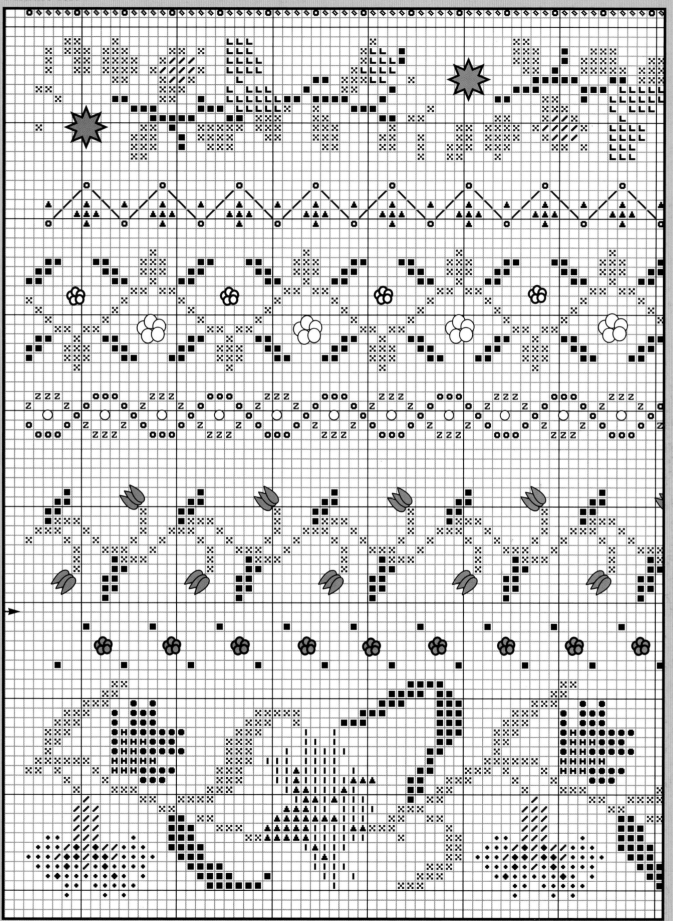

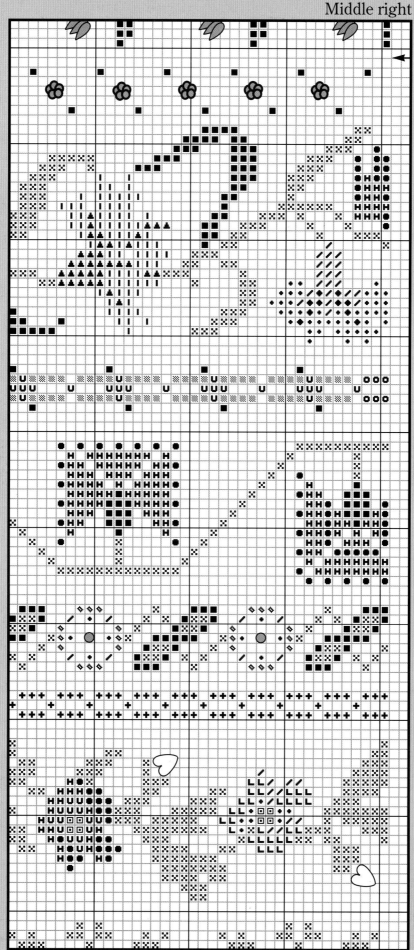

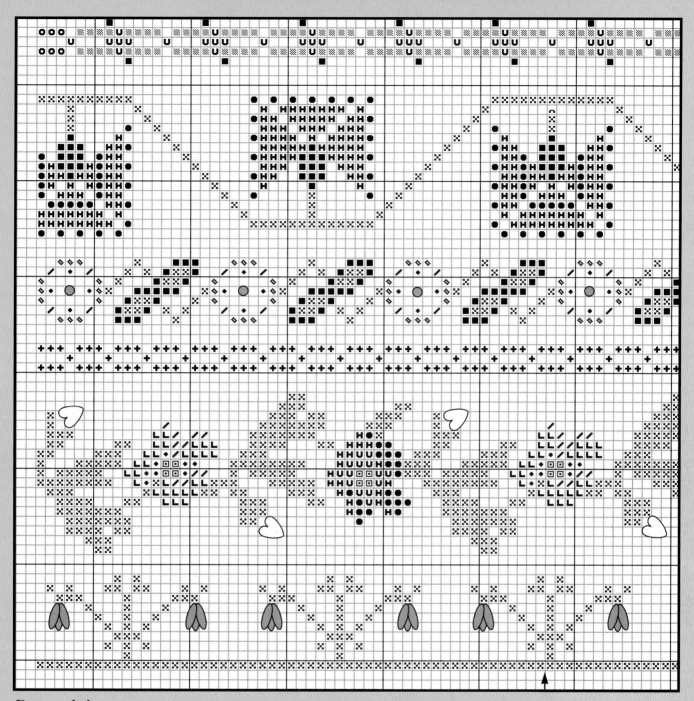

Bottom left

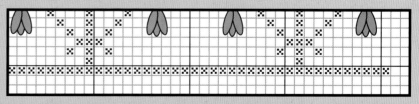

Bottom right

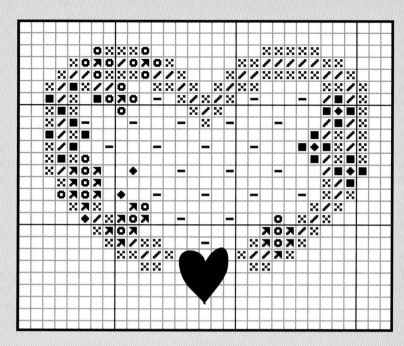

Wildflower Heart

Stitch Count: 27 x 23

Fabric: Linen, 28 count, antique white

Mill Hill Beads			
	SYMBOL	ATT W/FLOSS	#PKGS
479	✦	White	1
2011	◆	White	1
62012	↗	White	1
62034	■	White	1
62037	✿	White	1
62046	–	White	1
65270	✕	White	1
40161	UWT	White	1

Mill Hill Treasures			
	SYMBOL	ATT W/BEAD/FLOSS	#PKGS
12215	♥	40161/White	1

Home Sweet Home

Stitch Count: 27 x 23

Fabric: Linen, 28 count, antique white

DMC Floss	
	XS
501	✧
3752	·

Mill Hill Beads			
	SYMBOL	ATT W/FLOSS	#PKGS
123	◻	White	1
332	✦	White	1
556	◢	White	1
2014	■	White	1
62012	✿	White	1
62023	◆	White	1
62041	✚	White	1
62043	✕	White	1
40161	UWT	White	1

Mill Hill Treasures			
	SYMBOL	ATT W/BEAD/FLOSS	#PKGS
12192	▨	40161/White	1

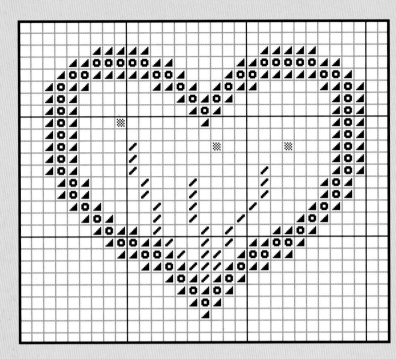

Pink Lace Heart

Stitch Count: 27 x 23

Fabric: Linen, 28 count, antique white

Mill Hill Beads			
	SYMBOL	ATT W/FLOSS	#PKGS
3005	◢	White	1
40161	UWT	White	1
62033	◘	White	1
65270	╱	White	1

Mill Hill Treasures			
	SYMBOL	ATT W/BEAD/FLOSS	#PKGS
12157	▨	40161/White	3

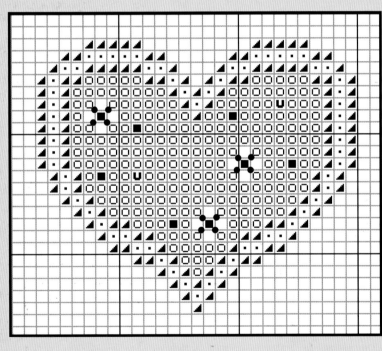

Denim Lace Heart

Stitch Count: 27 x 23

Fabric: Linen, 28 count, antique white

Note: Attach the butterfly in the open space at the top of the heart. Use one strand of ecru floss and go over the butterfly twice, once on each side of the body.

DMC Floss	
	XS
3752	◻

Mill Hill Beads			
	SYMBOL	ATT W/FLOSS	#PKGS
123	▪	Ecru	1
557	◼	Ecru	1
40123	●	Ecru/bead loops(10)	1
62043	◢	Ecru	1

Mill Hill Treasures			
	SYMBOL	ATT W/BEAD/FLOSS	#PKGS
12117	U	40123/Ecru	1
12122	*see note	/Ecru	1

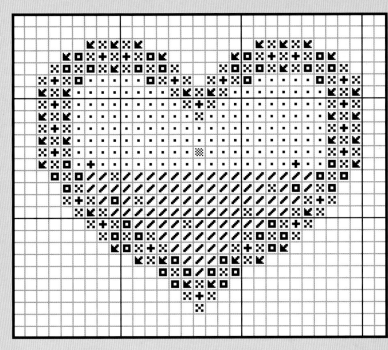

Meadow Heart

Stitch Count: 27 x 23

Fabric: Linen, 28 count, antique white

DMC Floss	
	XS
501	✐
3752	▪

Mill Hill Beads			
	SYMBOL	ATT W/FLOSS	#PKGS
330	+	White	1
3005	▫	White	1
40161	UWT	White	1
62033	▨	White	1
65270	◤	White	1

Mill Hill Treasures			
	SYMBOL	ATT W/BEAD/FLOSS	#PKGS
12216	▨	40161/White	1

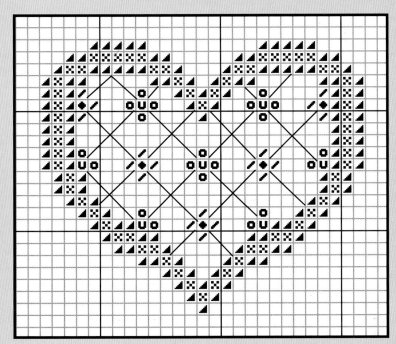

Golden Lattice

Stitch Count: 27 x 23

Fabric: Linen, 28 count, cream

DMC Floss	
	LS
5282	╱

Mill Hill Beads			
	SYMBOL	ATT W/FLOSS	#PKGS
123	▨	Ecru	1
553	▫	Ecru	1
557	◢	Ecru	1
2011	◆	Ecru	1
62012	U	Ecru	1
62034	✐	Ecru	1

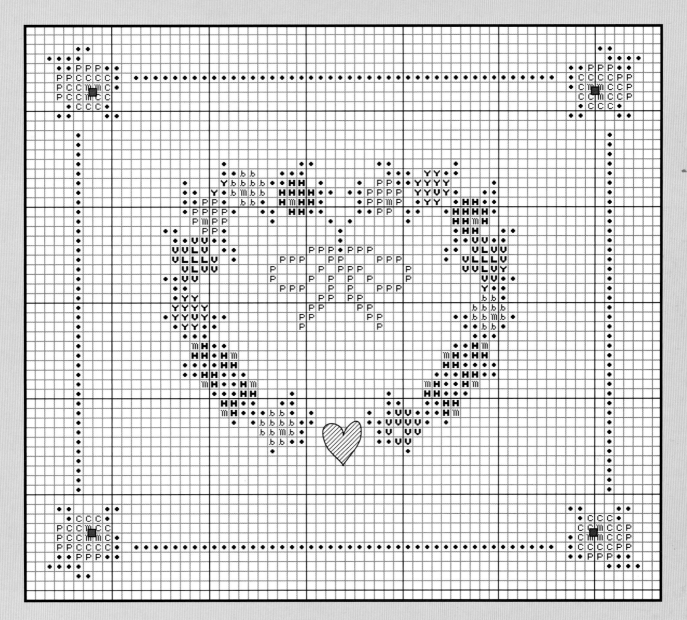

Victorian Heart Pillow

Stitch Count: 62 x 56

Fabric: Linen, 28 count, antique ivory

Mill Hill Beads			
	SYMBOL	ATT W/FLOSS	#PKGS
2019	Y	727	1
2025	U	3042	1
3020	H	315	1
3051	P	224	1
40252	b	793	1
45270	•	503	1
60168	L	340	1

DMC Floss	
	XS
224	C
315	m

Mill Hill Treasures			
	SYMBOL	ATT W/BEAD/FLOSS	#PKGS
12068	■	40252/793	1
13029	♡	/315	2

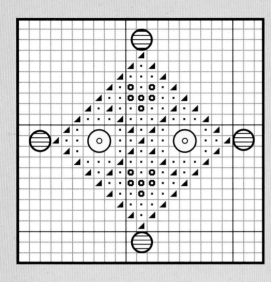

Mini Pearl Motif

Stitch Count: 21 x 21

Fabric: Linen, 28 count, cream

Mill Hill Beads

	SYMBOL	ATT W/FLOSS	#PKGS
2021	◢	Ecru	1
3019	✿	Ecru	1
3021	▪	Ecru	1
40161	UWT	Ecru	1

Mill Hill Treasures

	SYMBOL	ATT W/BEAD/FLOSS	#PKGS
13010	⊙	40161/Ecru	1
13017	⊜	/Ecru	2

Floral Heart

Stitch Count: 31 x 31

Fabric: Linen, 28 count, antique white

DMC Floss

	XS
501	◢
502	L
503	▽

Mill Hill Beads

	SYMBOL	ATT W/FLOSS	#PKGS
2012	▪	White	1
2002	✿	White	1
168	✖	White	1
252	◆	White	1
553	╲	White	1
40161	UWT	White	1

Mill Hill Treasures

	SYMBOL	ATT W/BEAD/FLOSS	#PKGS
12204	①	/310	1
12150	②	40161/White	2
12152	③	40161/White	1
12149	④	40161/White	1
12137	⑤	40161/White	1
12155	⑥	40161/White	1
12008	⑦	40161/White	1
12143	⑧	40161/White	3
12018	⑨	40161/White	1
12209	⑩	40161/White	1

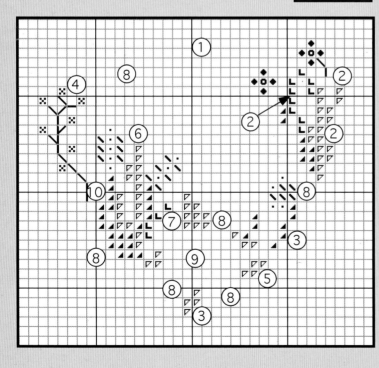

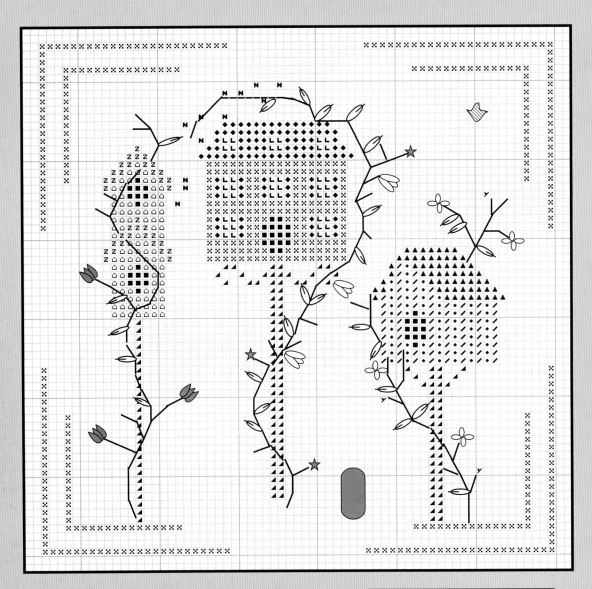

Birdhouses

Stitch Count: 65 x 65

Fabric: Linen, 28 count, antique white

Mill Hill Treasures

	SYMBOL	ATT W/BEAD/FLOSS	#PKGS
12051	✥	40161/Ecru	1
12147	✤	40161/Ecru	2
12148	★	40161/Ecru	2
12153	◍	40161/Ecru	3
12030	♈	145/224	1
12119	▮	/Ecru	1

DMC Floss

	XS	BS	FFK	DC
Ecru	L			
224	✦			
320		⌐		⬭
744	△		Y	
898	◣			
926	⬚			

Mill Hill Beads

	SYMBOL	ATT W/FLOSS	#PKGS
62023	▲	Ecru	1
3027	◆	Ecru	1
3018	╱	Ecru	1
3014	Z	Ecru	1
3002	■	Ecru	1
145	N	224	1
40161	UWT	Ecru	1

Graph 1: Foundation Stitching

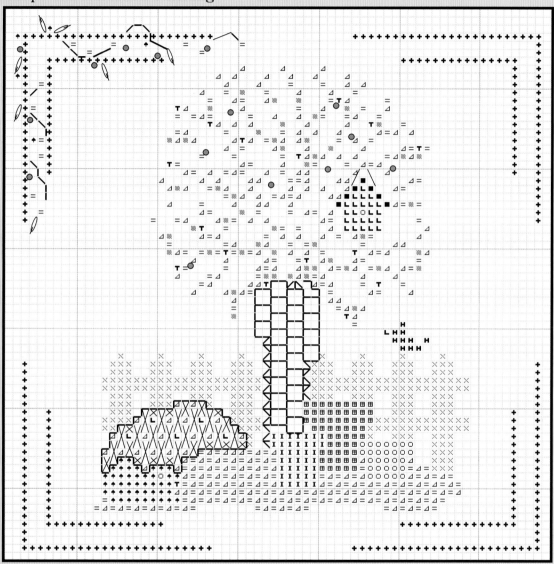

Backyard Apple Tree

Stitch Count: 67 x 67

Fabric: Linen, 28 count, antique white

Note: Rabbit's ears consist on 13 beads on each loop.

See page 40 for Graph 2.

DMC Floss	XS	UX	SX	DC	FK	LS
840⟩ 839⟩	▩		☐			
355	⊞					
320⟩ 367⟩	◢	✕				╱
320				◗		
926	✚					
927	✕					
744	∟				○	
3350					●	

39

Graph 2: Additional Beads/Treasures

Mill Hill Beads			
	SYMBOL	**ATT W/FLOSS**	**#PKGS**
40123	✚	Ecru	1
40123	● ●	Ecru/bead loops(3)	
40123	*see note	Ecru/bead loops(13)	
40252	○	Ecru/bead loops(6)	1
358	▢	926	1
330	■	840	1
40332	=	320	1
42028	I	840	1
2012	H	Ecru	1
62033	T	Ecru	1
40161	**UWT**	Ecru	1

Mill Hill Treasures			
	SYMBOL	**ATT W/BEAD/FLOSS**	**#PKGS**
12034	⬔	40161/Ecru	1
12121	⬠	/3350	1
12148	★	40161/Ecru	2
12147	☆	40161/Ecru	1
12149	✸	40161/Ecru	2

Graph 1: Foundation Stitching

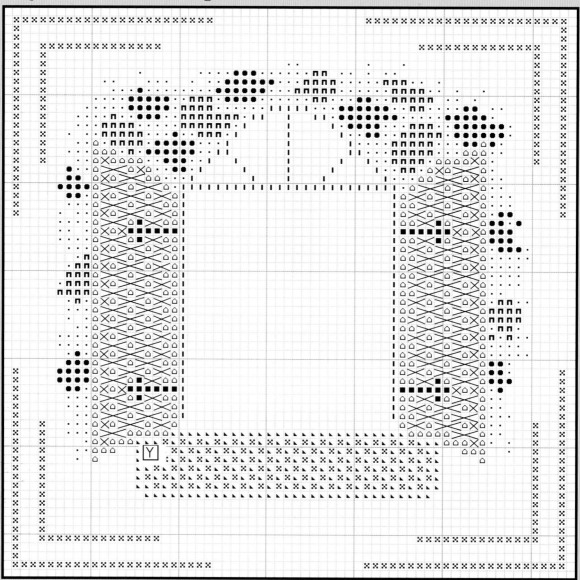

Window Box

Stitch Count: 70 x 70

Fabric: Linen, 28 count, antique white

DMC Floss				
	XS	**BS**	**UX**	**FFK**
612	●			
745				Y
828				●
3022	⌐			
3024	·			
3051		⌐		
3726	✖			
3768			✕	

Graph 2: Additional Beads/Treasures

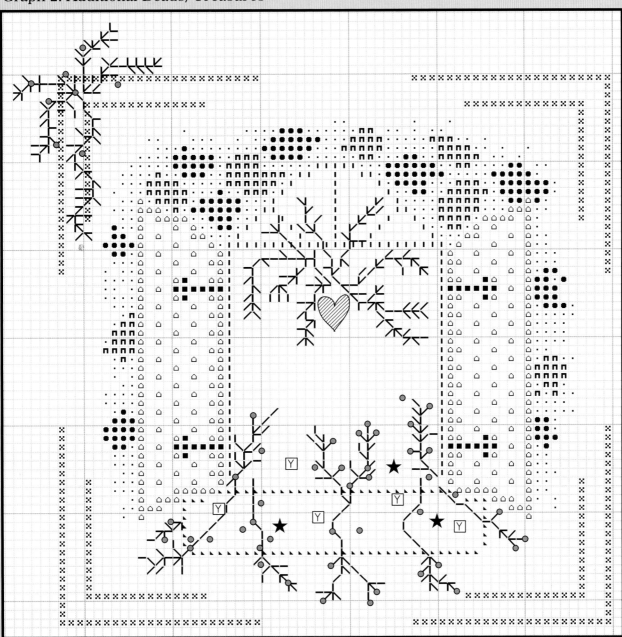

Mill Hill Beads			
	SYMBOL	ATT W/FLOSS	#PKGS
330	■	Ecru	1
3017	I	Ecru	1
3028	⌂	3768	2
40161	UWT	Ecru	1
42012	◣	3726	1

Mill Hill Treasures			
	SYMBOL	ATT W/BEAD/FLOSS	#PKGS
12067	♡	/225	1
13004	★	40161/Ecru	1

Cottage

Stitch Count: 67 x 66

Fabric: Linen, 28 count, antique white

DMC Floss						
	XS	**BS**	**FFK**	**DC**	**SX**	**UX**
309			▣			
501	ℕ	⌐		◊		
502	**Z**	∨				
744			◼			
746	✕				✳	
776			∟			
839	╱	⌐				
310		✕				
840	✚					✗
839⟩840⟩	∪					
842	▫					
932			✦			
3688			◹			

Mill Hill Beads			
	SYMBOL	**ATT W/FLOSS**	**#PKGS**
2012	●	309	1
2025	↗	3688	1
3024	▼	840	1
42029	▮	501	1
40161	**UWT**	746	1
62056	■	839	1
62046	=	746	1
62048	✦	776	1

Mill Hill Treasures			
	SYMBOL	**ATT W/BEAD/FLOSS**	**#PKGS**
12008	✿	40161/746	1
12147	★	40161/746	1
12149	✸	40161/746	1
13006	Ⓐ	40161/746	1

Cottage Door

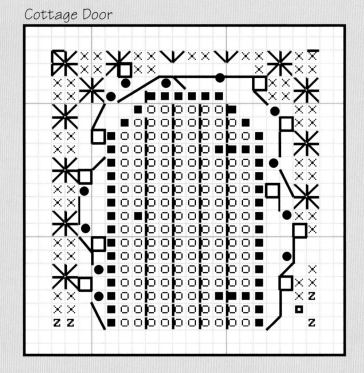

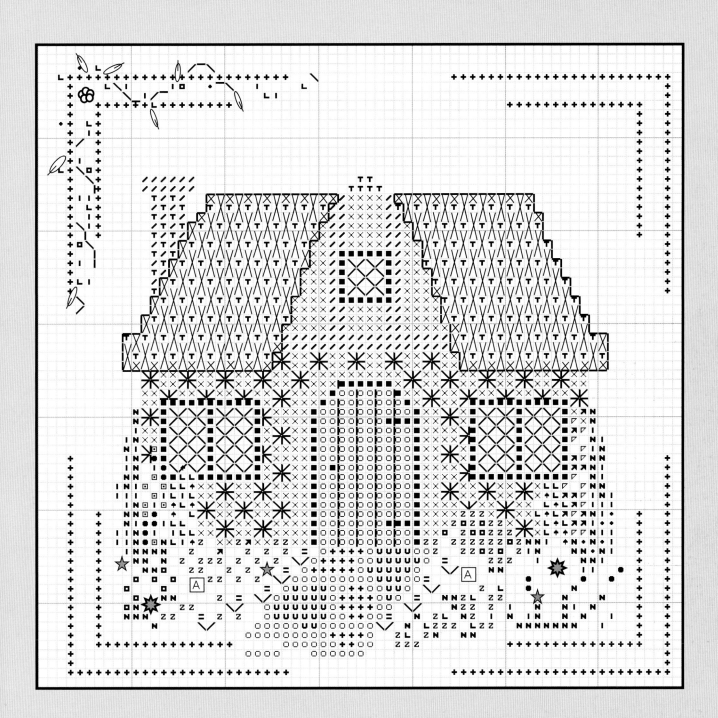

Love Is

Stitch Count: 71 x 57

Fabric: Linen, 28 count, antique white

Note: Refer to graph for treasure placement.

DMC Floss

	XS	BS	FK
223	╱		●
224	U	⌐	
340	=		
502	▢		
794	·		
3041	N		
3350	Z		

Mill Hill Beads

	SYMBOL	ATT W/FLOSS	#PKGS
2025	▬	3041	1
3021	⠭	Ecru	1
3051	◢	224	1
62041	Y	744	1
62046	I	794	1
45270	◆	502	1
40161	UWT	Ecru	1

Mill Hill Treasures

	SYMBOL	ATT W/BEAD/FLOSS	#PKGS
12209	●	40161/Ecru	2
12204	✿	/310(1 strand)	1
12187	✜	40161/Ecru	2
13001	○	40161/Ecru	1
13002	●	40161/Ecru	1
12116	✸	40161/Ecru	1
12212	✺	40161/Ecru	1
12208	*see note	40161/Ecru	2
12115	*see note	40161/Ecru	1

May All the Love

Stitch Count: 48 x 57

Fabric: Linen, 32 count, antique white

Mill Hill Beads			
	SYMBOL	ATT W/FLOSS	#PKGS
168	U	White	1
252	T	White	1
553	✦	White	1
2002	▫	White	1
40161	UWT	White	1

DMC Floss		
	XS	BS
223		⌐
502	✖	
503	•	

Mill Hill Treasures			
	SYMBOL	ATT W/BEAD/FLOSS	#PKGS
12213	🌷	40161/White	1
12155	🌷	40161/White	1
12143	🍃	40161/White	3
12149	✿	40161/White	2
12013	✴	40161/White	1
12151	✾	40161/White	3
12152	✳	40161/White	1
12114	♥	40161/White	1

Graph 1: Foundation Stitching

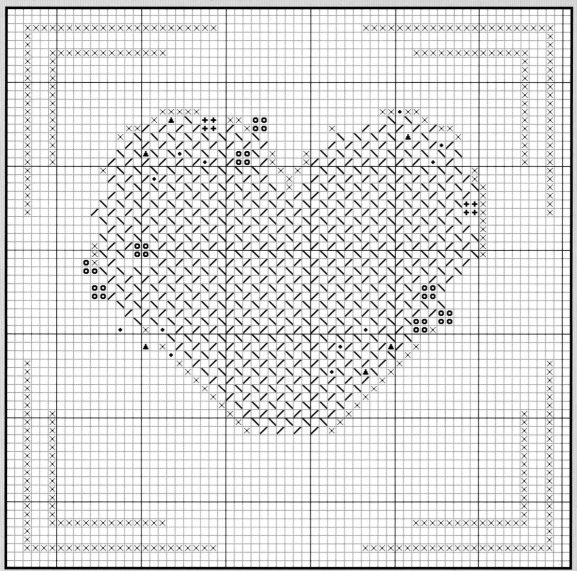

Alicia's Heart

Stitch Count: 65 x 65

Fabric: Linen, 28 count, antique white

DMC Floss				
	XS	AL	LS	DC
224		⌐		
3816	⤫		╲	⬭

Mill Hill Beads			
	SYMBOL	ATT W/FLOSS	#PKGS
62012	✦✦	224/bead posie (5)	1
62041	♣	White/bead posie (5)	1
3021	∷	White/bead loops (7)	1
62046/3021	◦◦	White/bead posie (4/1)	1
40161	UWT	White	1
40252/40161	✦	White/bead posie (4/1)	1

Graph 2: Additional Beads/Treasures

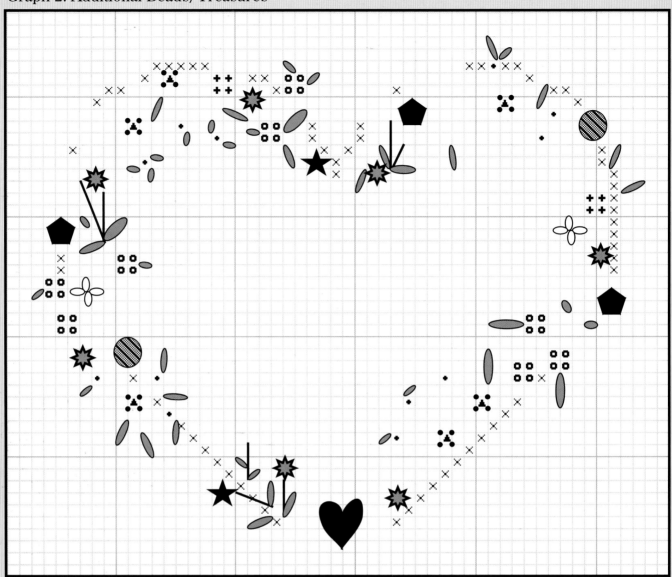

Mill Hill Treasures			
	SYMBOL	**ATT W/BEAD/FLOSS**	**#PKGS**
13006	✸	40161/White	2
12099	♥	40161/224	1
12011	✤	40161/White	2
12209	⬠	40161/White	2
12210	◉	40161/White	1
12138	★	40161/White	1

A Day in the Country

Stitch Count: 42 x 112

Fabric: Linen, 28 count, antique ivory

Mill Hill Beads			
	SYMBOL	ATT W/FLOSS	#PKGS
3005	C	Ecru	1
3007	•	927	1
40123	N	Ecru-2 beads per	1

DMC Floss				
	XS	BS	SX	SS
407	·			
523	T			
612	I			
927	x			
950	o			

Mill Hill Treasures			
	SYMBOL	ATT W/BEAD/FLOSS	#PKGS
12212		3005/Ecru	4
12092		/Ecru	1
12216		/Ecru	2

Top

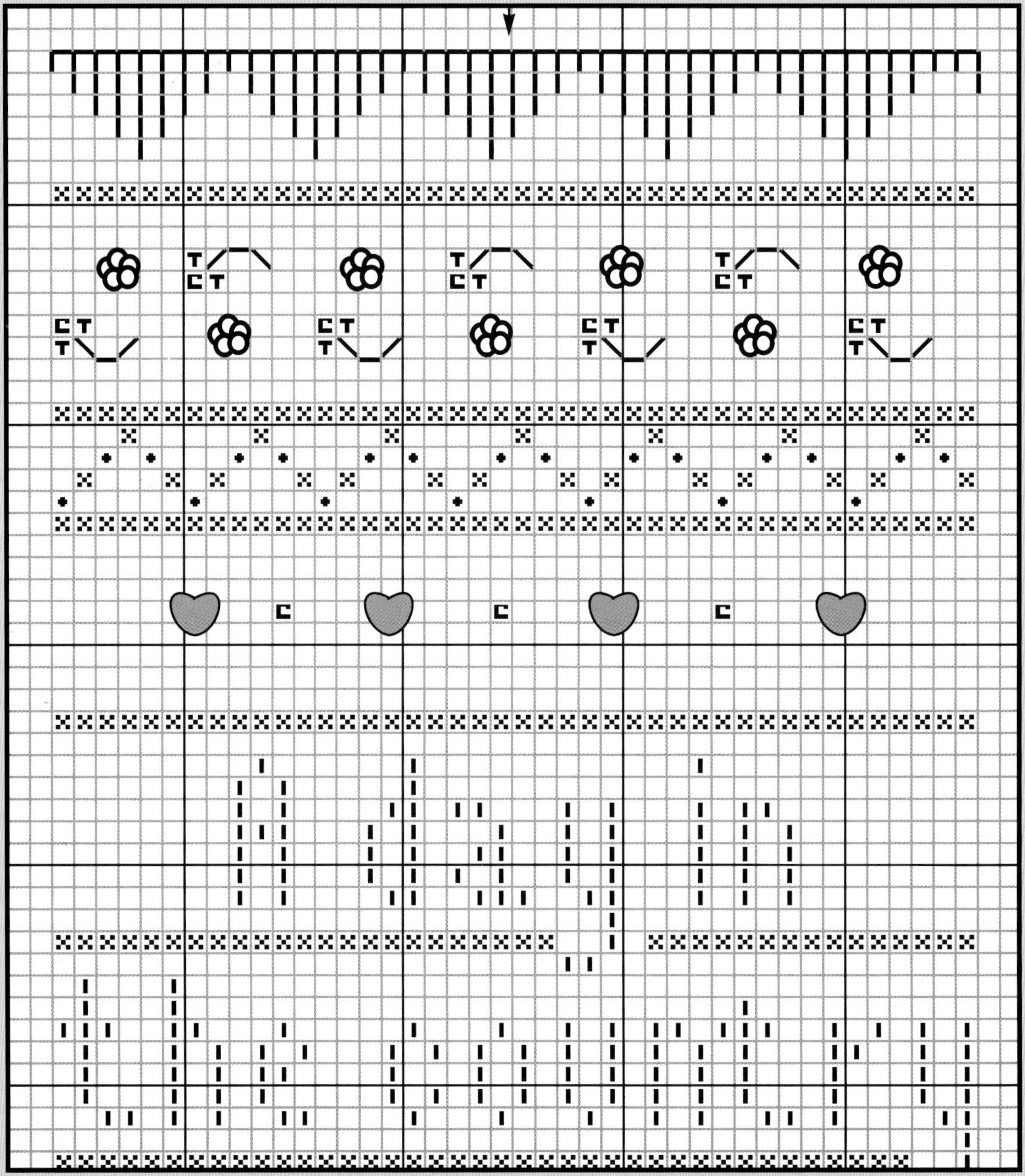

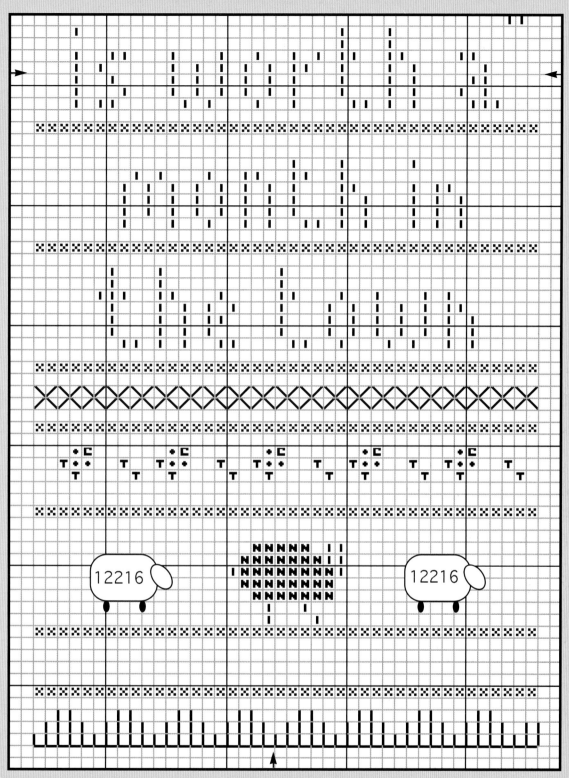

Bottom

Acorn Sampler

Stitch Count: 115 x 175

Fabric: Linen, 25 count, driftwood

Note: For Herringbone border, work back and forth in rows. Begin four threads down from the upper left corner of the section (top row is already charted). Work from top to bottom in the following sequence of floss: 315, 3740, 3787, 3750, 3740, and 315. Some compensation may be necessary at the end of the row. Refer to graph for treasure placement.

DMC Floss			
	XS	SS	HB
3787	╱		
3750	◢		
646	I	▬▬	
315	·		
3740			*see note
3024	UWB-UWT		

Mill Hill Beads			
	SYMBOL	ATT W/FLOSS	#PKGS
556	◉	3024	2
3013	✖	3024	5
3011	I	3024	1
3025	◆	3024	4
3036	∪	3024	1
40161	UWT	3024	1

Mill Hill Treasures			
	SYMBOL	ATT W/BEAD/FLOSS	#PKGS
12199	◁	/3024	10
13002	✸	40161/3024	1
13024	◈	/3024	7
12196	*see note	40161/3024	1

Top left

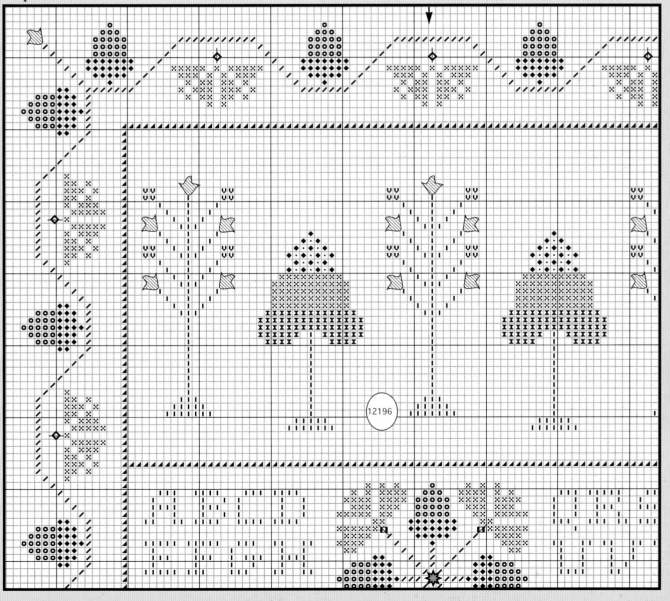

Top right

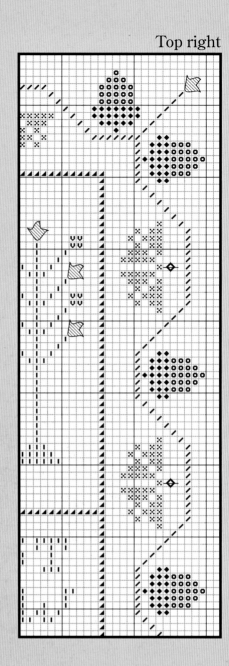

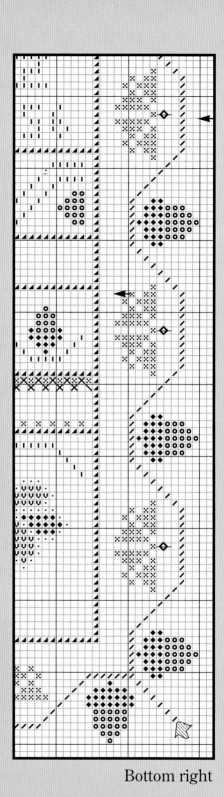

Bottom right

DMC Floss			
	XS	**SS**	**HB**
3787	✎		
3750	◢		
646	▮	〰	
315	▪		
3740			*see note
3024	**UWB-UWT**		

Mill Hill Beads			
	SYMBOL	**ATT W/FLOSS**	**#PKGS**
556	✿	3024	2
3013	✖	3024	5
3011	✗	3024	1
3025	◆	3024	4
3036	∪	3024	1
40161	**UWT**	3024	1

SATIN STITCH BORDER

HERRINGBONE BORDER

START HERE

Bottom left

Mill Hill Treasures			
	SYMBOL	ATT W/BEAD/FLOSS	#PKGS
12199	🦢	/3024	10
13002	✸	40161/3024	1
13024	◈	/3024	7
12196	*see note	40161/3024	1

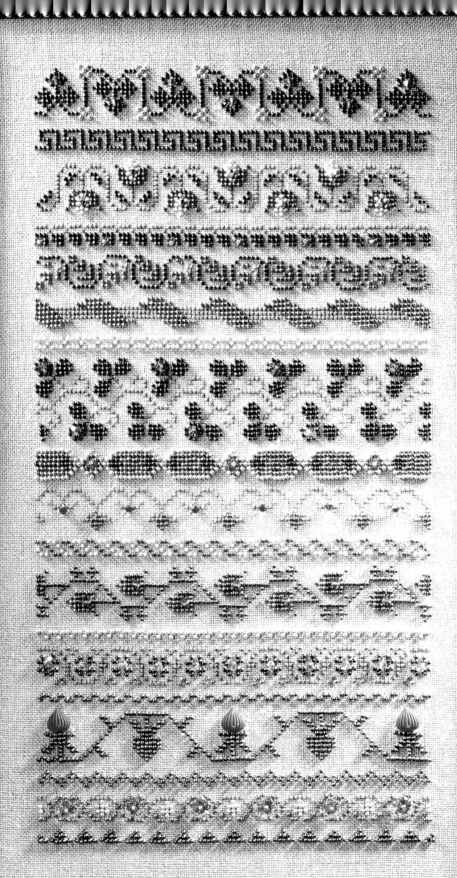

Antique Borders

Stitch Count: 95 x 181

Fabric: Linen, 28 count, natural

DMC Floss	
	XS
3051	✖

Mill Hill Beads			
	SYMBOL	ATT W/FLOSS	#PKGS
221	✚	642	2
330	♣	642	2
557	◘	642	1
3002	⊗	642	1
3003	❑	642	1
3014	■	642	1
62031	◆	642	1

Mill Hill Treasures			
	SYMBOL	ATT W/BEAD/FLOSS	#PKGS
12188	★	40557/642	5
13009	●	3002/642	3
12190	★	40557/642	3
13027	◆	/642	3
12010	✸	40557/642	6
12207	♥	/814	3
13018	○	/642	4
13029	◇	/642	3
13034	◆	/642	2

Top left

59

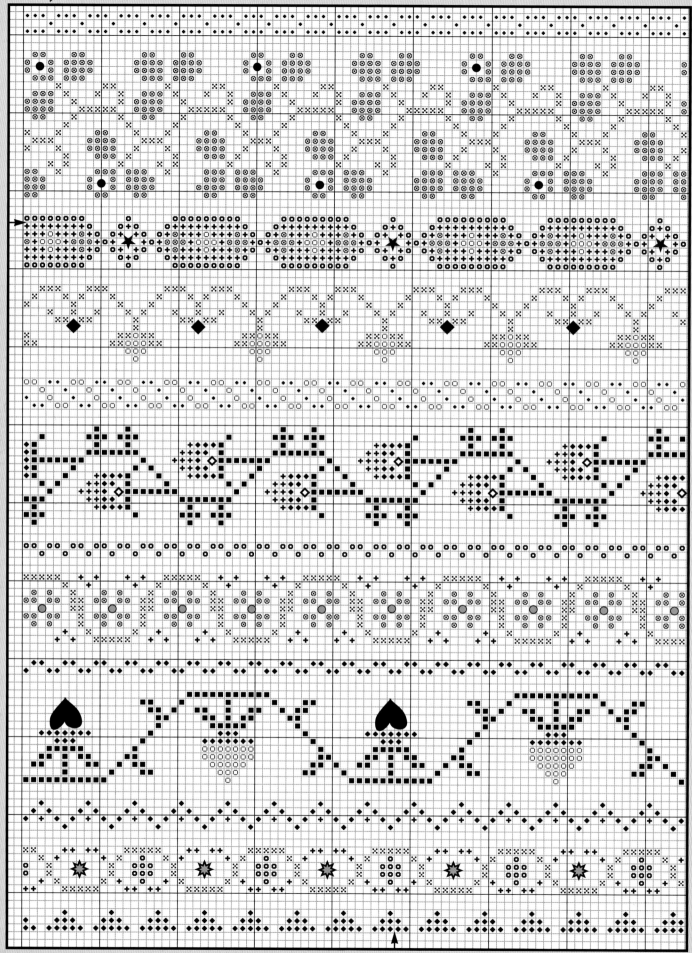

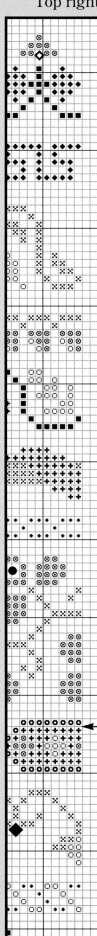

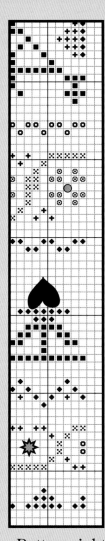

Bottom right

DMC Floss

	XS
3051	✖

Mill Hill Beads

	SYMBOL	ATT W/FLOSS	#PKGS
221	✚	642	2
330	✚	642	2
557	▫	642	1
3002	⊗	642	1
3003	▢	642	1
3014	■	642	1
62031	◆	642	1

Mill Hill Treasures

	SYMBOL	ATT W/BEAD/FLOSS	#PKGS
12188	★	40557/642	5
13009	●	3002/642	3
12190	★	40557/642	3
13027	◆	/642	3
12010	✹	40557/642	6
12207	♥	/814	3
13018	●	/642	4
13029	◇	/642	3
13034	◆	/642	2

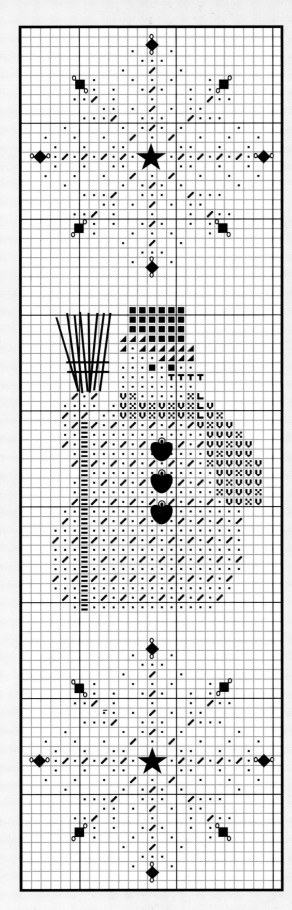

Snowman Bell Pull

Stitch Count: 25 x 88

Fabric: Banding, 27 count, blue

Special Instructions: Stitch the broom with metallic thread. After taking the long vertical stitches, "tie" across the broom straw with horizontal stitches as charted.

Note: Attach treasure at bottom of bell pull.

Kreinik		
	LS	#SPOOLS
098 #8 Braid	/	1

Mill Hill Beads			
	SYMBOL	ATT W/FLOSS	#PKGS
81	◢	310	1
2014	■	310	1
423	T	321	1
42013	✖	321	1
2020	U	3818	1
479	·	White	2
42010	/	White	1
556	=	White	1
367	L	321	1
40161	UWT	White	1

Mill Hill Treasures			
	SYMBOL	ATT W/BEAD/FLOSS	#PKGS
12165	★	40161/White	1
12077	♥	40161/White	2
13023	⚷	40161/White	6
12162	*see note	40161/White	1

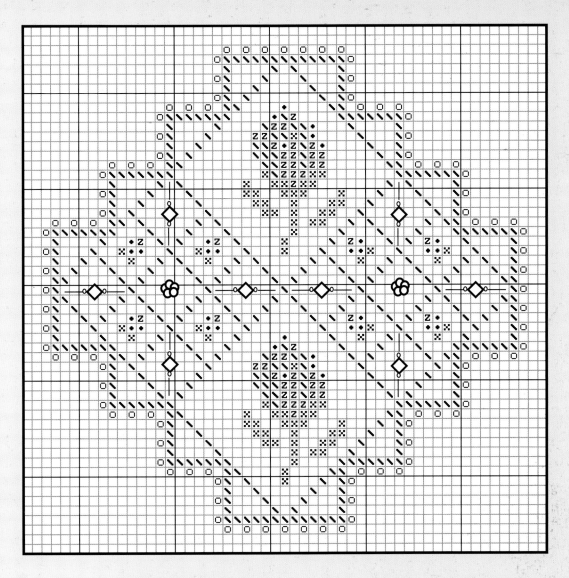

Crystal Fantasy Box

Stitch Count: 51 x 51

Fabric: Aida, 18 count, pink

Mill Hill Beads			
	SYMBOL	ATT W/FLOSS	#PKGS
40553	•	819	1
42010	◣	Ecru	1
42012	z	819	1
42018	▢	819	1
45270	▓	502	1

Mill Hill Treasures			
	SYMBOL	ATT W/BEAD/FLOSS	#PKGS
12152	✿	42010/Ecru	1
13031	◇	42010/819	3

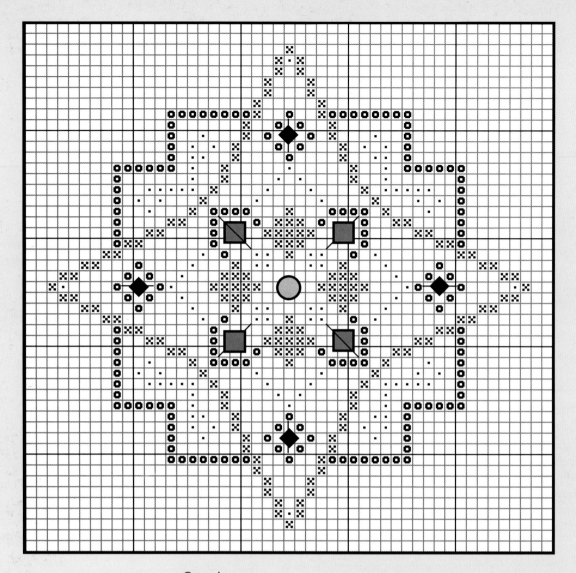

Starburst

Stitch Count: 45 x 45

Fabric: Linen, 28 count, antique white

Mill Hill Treasures			
	SYMBOL	ATT W/FLOSS	#PKGS
13023	■	White	2
13029	◆	White	2
13037	○	White	2

Mill Hill Beads			
	SYMBOL	ATT W/FLOSS	#PKGS
2024	✗	White	1
151	●	White	1
2010	·	White	1

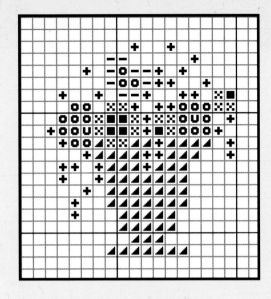

Floral Vase Brooch

Stitch Count: 16 x 18

Fabric: Linen, 28 count, ivory

Mill Hill Beads			
	SYMBOL	ATT W/FLOSS	#PKGS
556	◢	Ecru	1
62033	✖	Ecru	1
62034	▢	Ecru	1
332	✚	Ecru	1
3033	■	Ecru	1
2011	∪	Ecru	1
123	—	Ecru	1

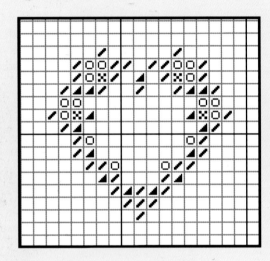

Mini Heart Box

Stitch Count: 15 x 14

Fabric: Linen, 28 count, antique white

Mill Hill Beads			
	SYMBOL	ATT W/FLOSS	#PKGS
65270	✦	White	1
62033	▢	White	1
62012	✖	White	1
3037	◢	White	1

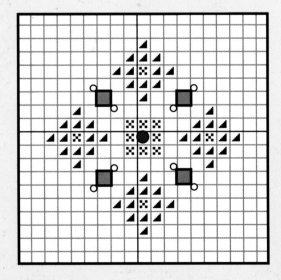

Mini Motif Box

Stitch Count: 15 x 15

Fabric: Linen, 28 count, confederate grey

Mill Hill Beads			
	SYMBOL	ATT W/FLOSS	#PKGS
2022	✖	927	1
3004	◢	927	1

Mill Hill Treasures			
	SYMBOL	ATT W/BEAD/FLOSS	#PKGS
13029	▪	2022/927	2
13014	●	/927	1

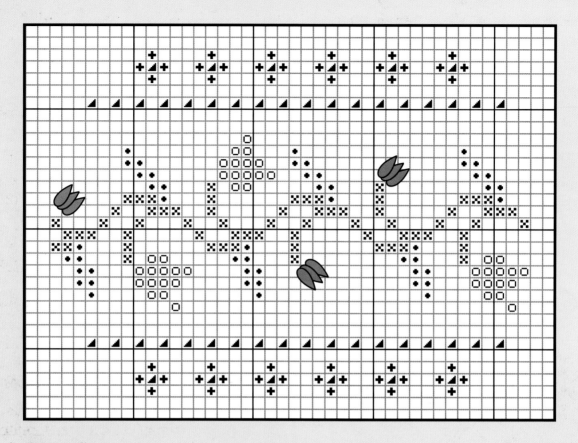

Petite Fleur

Stitch Count: 40 x 29

Fabric: Linen, 32 count, cream

DMC Floss	
	XS
778	✦
502	✖

Mill Hill Beads			
	SYMBOL	ATT W/FLOSS	#PKGS
42024	▢	Ecru	1
42027	◢	Ecru	1
45270	✦	Ecru	1

Mill Hill Treasures			
	SYMBOL	ATT W/BEAD/FLOSS	#PKGS
12158	🌷	42027/Ecru	3

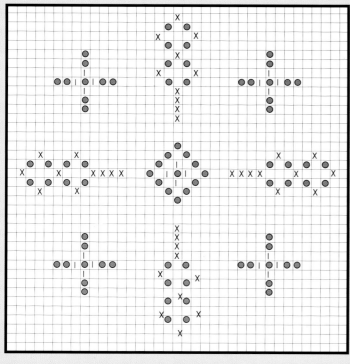

Aqua Ice Box

Stitch Count: 35 x 35

Fabric: Linen, 28 count, antique white

Note: After stitching, attach bugle beads and clusters to vertical and horizontal stems as follows:

cluster of four champagne petite (42027)

cluster of one aqua ice med. bugle (82054), one champagne petite (42027), one crystal aqua (2017)

cluster of one tapestry teal petite (42029), one crystal aqua (2017), one tapestry teal petite (42029)

Add bugle beads and clusters to diagonal stems as follows:

ice short bugle (72010)

aqua ice med. bugle (82054)

cluster on each side of aqua ice bugle: one champagne petite (42027), two crystal aqua (2017), one champagne petite (42047)

cluster of three champagne petite (42047), one crystal aqua (2017)

Add clusters to the center area as follows:

cluster of one champagne petite (42047), three crystal aqua (2017), one champagne petite (42047)

cluster of three crystal aqua (2017)

cluster of one tapestry teal (42029), two champagne petite (42047), one tapestry teal (42029)

working from the center cluster, one tapestry teal (42029), two champagne petite (42027), one tapestry teal (42029)

Mill Hill Beads			
	SYMBOL	ATT W/FLOSS	#PKGS
2017	X	White	1
42029	○	White	1
2010	l	White	1
42027	*see note	White	1
82054	*see note	White	1
72010	*see note	White	1

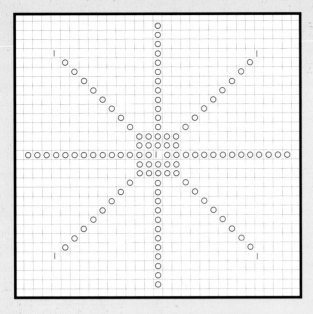

Pink Crystal Box

Stitch Count: 31 x 31

Fabric: Linen, 28 count, antique white

Note: After stitching is complete, add bugle beads and clusters to the horizontal and vertical stems as follows:

ice short bugle (72010)	
dusty rose short bugle (72005)	
cluster of one crystal pink petites (42018), one ice (2010), one crystal pink (42018)	

Add bugle beads and clusters to the diagonal stems as follows:

cluster of three crystal pink petites (42018)	
one ice (2010), one dusty rose short bugle (72005), one ice (2010)	
cluster of three crystal pink petites (42018), one ice (2010)	
dusty rose short bugle (72005)	
cluster of two ice (2010)	

Add clusters to the center area as follows:

(cluster of two crystal pink (42018), one ice (2010)

Mill Hill Beads			
	SYMBOL	ATT W/FLOSS	#PKGS
2018	○	White	1
2010			White	1
72010	*see note	White	1
72005	*see note	White	1
42018	*see note	White	1

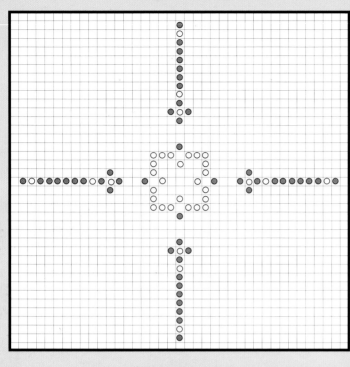

Blue Ice Box

Stitch Count: 37 x 37

Fabric: Linen, 28 count, antique white

Note: After stitching is complete, add bugle beads and clusters to the horizontal and vertical stems as follows:

━●●●●━	cluster of four crystal blue (2026)
━▭▭━	sapphire med. bugle (80168)
━○●●●●○	cluster of four crystal blue (2026), one ice (2010)
━▭━	ice short bugle (72010)

Add bugle beads and clusters to the diagonal stems as follows:

━○▭▭━	one sapphire med. bugle (80168), one ice (2010)
○━▭▭━○	one ice (2010), one sapphire med. bugle (80168), one ice (2010)
━▭━	ice short bugle (72010)
✦	cluster of one crystal blue (2026), one ice (2010), one crystal blue (2026)
✦	cluster of two crystal blue (2026)
✦	ice (2010)
━●●●━	cluster of three crystal blue (2026)
━▭●━	one ice short bugle (72010), one crystal blue (2026)
●●●●━	cluster of four crystal blue (2026)

Add clusters and pebble bead to the center area as follows:

━●○●━	cluster of one crystal blue (2026), one ice (2010), one crystal blue
ⓘⓅ	crystal pebble (05161)

Mill Hill Beads			
	SYMBOL	**ATT W/FLOSS**	**#PKGS**
2010	○	White	1
2026	●	White	1
80168	*see note	White	1
72010	*see note	White	1
05161	*see note	White	1

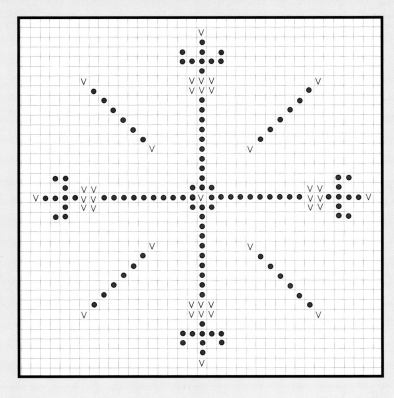

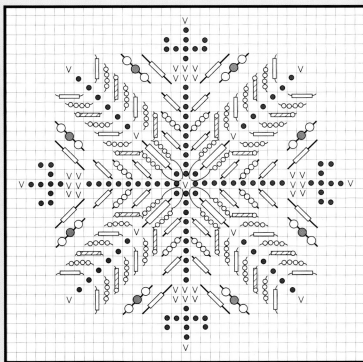

Crystalline Copper Box

Stitch Count: 35 x 35

Fabric: Linen, 28 count, antique white

Note: After stitching is complete, add bugle beads and clusters to the horizontal and vertical stems as follows:

⊏▭⊐ nutmeg short bugle (72053)

-○●○- cluster of one Victorian copper petite (42030), one mercury (283), one Victorian copper petite (42030)

-○○○- cluster of four Victorian copper petites (42030)

Add bugle beads and clusters to diagonal stems as follows:

◠▭◠ nutmeg short bugle (72053)

-○○○○ cluster of four Victorian copper petites (42030)

○▱▱ one ice short bugle (72010), one Victorian copper petite (42030)

Add clusters to center area as follows:

⌒ working from the center cluster, one Victorian copper petite (42030), three mercury (283)

Mill Hill Beads			
	SYMBOL	ATT W/FLOSS	#PKGS
42030	V	White	1
283	●	White	1
72053	*see note	White	1
72010	*see note	White	1

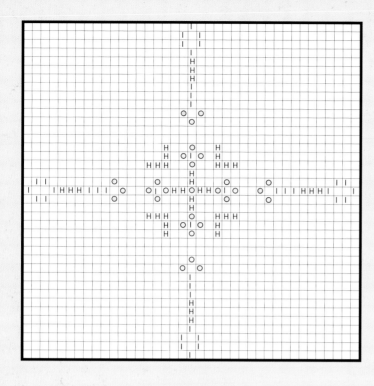

Crystalline Teal Box

Stitch Count: 39 x 39

Fabric: Linen, 28 count, antique white

Note: After stitching is complete, add bugle beads and clusters to the horizontal and vertical stems as follows:

- cluster of three tapestry teal petites (42029)

- cluster of four tapestry teal petites (42029)

- one ice short bugle (72010), one tapestry teal petite (42029)

- cluster of four ice petites (42010), one tapestry teal petite (42029)

- ice short bugle (72010)

- cluster of one ice petite (42010), four tapestry teal petites (42029)

Add bugle beads and clusters to the diagonal stems as follows:

- nutmeg short bugle (72053)

- heather mauve (2024)

- one ice short bugle (72010), one tapestry teal petite (42029)

- one nutmeg short bugle (72053), one tapestry teal petite (42029)

- cluster of four heather mauve (2024)

- tapestry teal petite (42029)

Add clusters to the center area as follows:

- cluster of four tapestry teal petites (42029)

- cluster of one tapestry teal petite (42029), two ice petites (42010), one tapestry teal petite (42029)

- over the top, place clusters of one tapestry teal petite (42029), two ice petites (42010), one tapestry teal petite

Mill Hill Beads			
	SYMBOL	ATT W/FLOSS	#PKGS
42029	●	White	1
2024	H	White	1
2010	I	White	1
72010	*see note	White	1
72053	*see note	White	1
42010	*see note	White	1

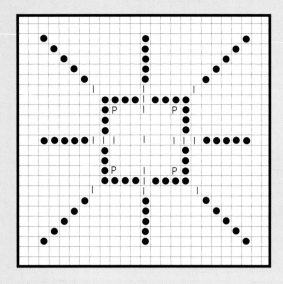

Golden Ice Box

Stitch Count: 33 x 33

Fabric: Linen, 28 count, antique white

Note: After stitching is complete, add bugle beads and clusters to the horizontal and vertical stems as follows:

▭	gold short bugle (72011)
●▭▭	one ice short bugle (72010), one Victorian gold petite (42011)
▭▭	one ice (2010), one gold short bugle (72011), one ice (2010)
●●	two clusters of two gold (557)
००००	cluster of four ice petites (42010)

Add bugle beads and clusters to the diagonal stems as follows:

◦◦◦◦	four Victorian gold petites (42011)
००००●	four ice petites (42010), one gold (557)
▭▭▭	ice short bugle (72010)

Add bugle beads and clusters to the center area as follows:

▭	gold short bugle (72011)
●●●●	four Victorian gold petites (42011)
⌒	working from the center, pick up three ice petites (42010), one Victorian gold petite (42011)

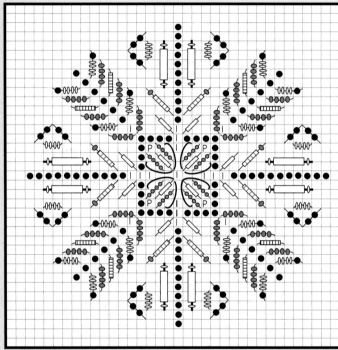

Mill Hill Beads			
	SYMBOL	**ATT W/FLOSS**	**#PKGS**
557	●	White	1
2010	I	White	1
42010	P	White	1
72011	*see note	White	1
72010	*see note	White	1
42011	*see note	White	1

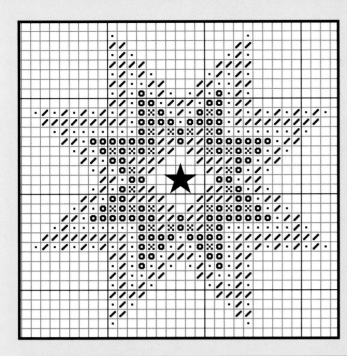

Star Box

Stitch Count: 33 x 33

Fabric: Linen, 28 count, antique white

DMC Floss	
	XS
White	⬭

Kreinik		
	HX	#SPOOLS
210 #8 Braid	✎	1

Mill Hill Treasures			
	SYMBOL	ATT W/BEAD/FLOSS	#PKGS
12161	★	2010/White	1

Mill Hill Beads			
	SYMBOL	ATT W/FLOSS	#PKGS
557	▪	White	1
2010	❌	White	1

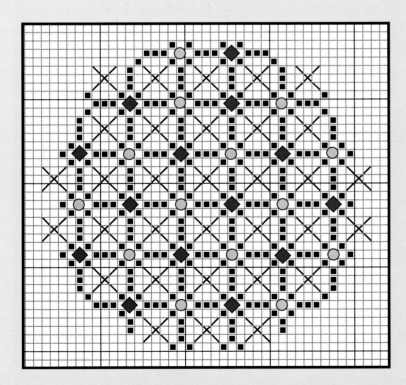

Background Maze Box

Stitch Count: 39 x 37

Fabric: Linen, 28 count, cream

Kreinik		
	LXS	#SPOOLS
002 #4 Braid	X	1

Mill Hill Treasures			
	SYMBOL	ATT W/FLOSS	#PKGS
13027	◆	Ecru	5
13022	●	Ecru	5

Mill Hill Beads			
	SYMBOL	ATT W/FLOSS	#PKGS
2001	■	Ecru	1

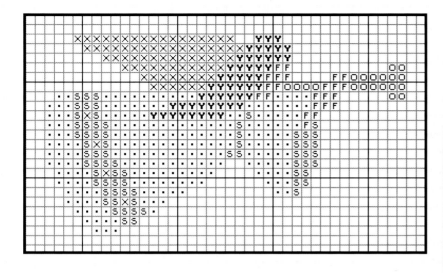

Blue Angel

Stitch Count: 38 x 21

Fabric: Perforated paper, 14 count, white

Mill Hill Beads			
	SYMBOL	**ATT W/FLOSS**	**#PKGS**
148	Y	White	1
145	F	White	1
557	O	White	1
2010	X	White	1
146	·	White	1
168	S	White	1

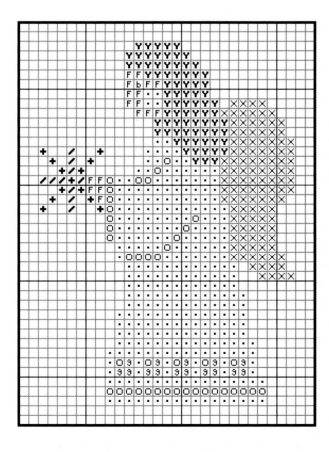

Pink Angel

Stitch Count: 27 x 38

Fabric: Perforated paper, 14 count, white

Mill Hill Beads			
	SYMBOL	**ATT W/FLOSS**	**#PKGS**
148	Y	White	1
145	F	White	1
2005	·	White	1
358	b	White	1
553	O	White	1
561	ɜ	White	1
479	X	White	1
557	╱	White	1
2010	+	White	1

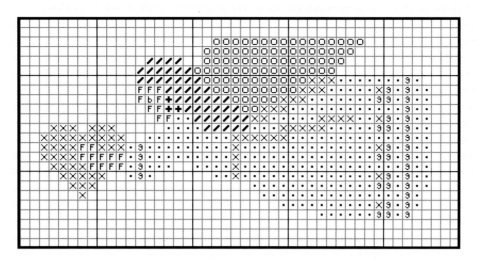

Flying Angel

Stitch Count: 41 x 19

Fabric: Perforated paper, 14 count, white

Mill Hill Beads			
	SYMBOL	ATT W/FLOSS	#PKGS
332	ɘ	Ecru	1
123	▪	Ecru	1
2012	✕	Ecru	1
275	✦	Ecru	1
145	F	Ecru	1
2005	✚	Ecru	1
557	▢	Ecru	1
358	Ƅ	Ecru	1

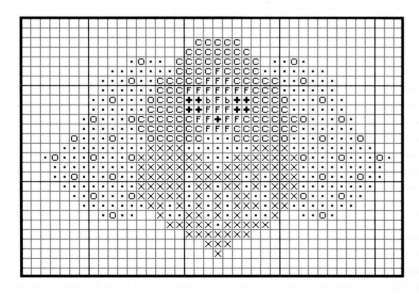

Joy Angel

Stitch Count: 37 x 23

Fabric: Perforated paper, 14 count, ivory

Mill Hill Beads			
	SYMBOL	ATT W/FLOSS	#PKGS
2012	✕	Ecru	1
123	▪	Ecru	1
275	C	Ecru	1
145	F	Ecru	1
2005	✚	Ecru	1
358	Ƅ	Ecru	1
557	▢	Ecru	1

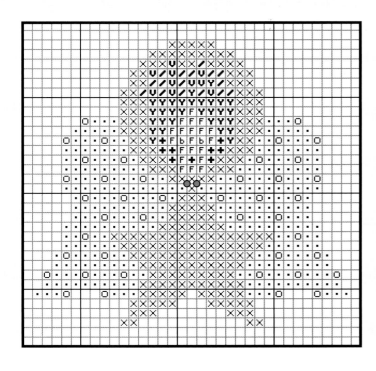

Star Angel

Stitch Count: 33 x 30

Fabric: Perforated paper, 14 count, white

DMC Floss	
	Bow
814	⚪

Mill Hill Beads			
	SYMBOL	**ATT W/FLOSS**	**#PKGS**
557	✕	White	1
148	Y	White	1
479	·	White	1
161	◻	White	1
2012	✒	White	1
332	∪	White	1
358	♭	White	1
145	F	White	1
2005	✚	White	1

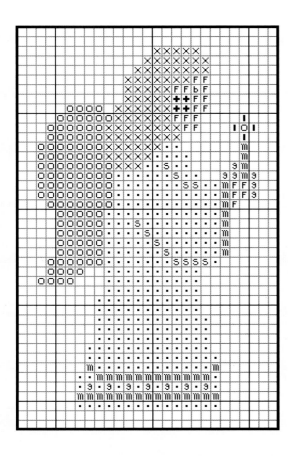

Candle Angel

Stitch Count: 23 x 37

Fabric: Perforated paper, 14 count, ivory

Mill Hill Beads			
	SYMBOL	**ATT W/FLOSS**	**#PKGS**
123	·	Ecru	1
2012	�	Ecru	1
332	϶	Ecru	1
557	◻	Ecru	1
145	F	Ecru	1
2005	✚	Ecru	1
358	♭	Ecru	1
275	✕	Ecru	1
2010	I	Ecru	1
556	ѕ	Ecru	1

Wedding Memories

Stitch Count: 154 x 200

Fabric: Linen, 27 count, cream

Special Instructions: Stitch the Kloster Blocks (KB) first. Attach pearl beads with Half-cross Stitch (HX) over the center two threads. Using the Large Alphabet on page 91, center couple's last name on the line indicated and stitch with DMC floss (739).

Center the first and middle names and backstitch with DMC floss (932). Using the Large Alphabet, center an initial in each box and stitch with pearl beads. Center date between the intersecting hearts and backstitch with DMC floss (932). Center the year and stitch in pearl beads.

To work flower loops, come up at the dots, pick up ten pearl beads, go down in the same hole, creating five loops around each flower. Do not pull too tight.

DMC Floss	XS	BS	ES	FSS	FS
Ecru			✳	▭	⌐┘
223	△				
502		⌐┘			
503	⬤				
739	T				
932		⌐┘			
3752	•				

DMC Perle Cotton	KB
Ecru #8	⫶⫶
Ecru #8	UU UU

Kreinik		XS	#SPOOLS
002 #4 Braid		◢	1

Mill Hill Beads	SYMBOL	ATT W/FLOSS	#PKGS
2006	b	Ecru	1
2007	✛	Ecru	1
2016	✖	502	2
2017	◻	932	2
3018	L	Ecru	2
3020	◻	Ecru	2
3021	○ ■	Ecru	9
3021	◼	Ecru/bead loops (10)	

Mill Hill Treasures	SYMBOL	ATT W/BEAD/FLOSS	#PKGS
13031	◇	/Ecru	3
12143	◗	/503	8
12086	♥	/Ecru	1
12092	♡	/Ecru	2
12214	♡	3021/Ecru	1

Top left

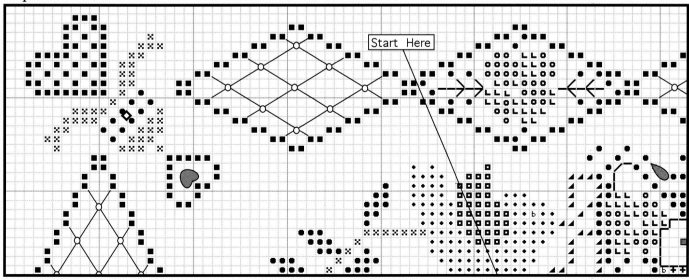

Top center

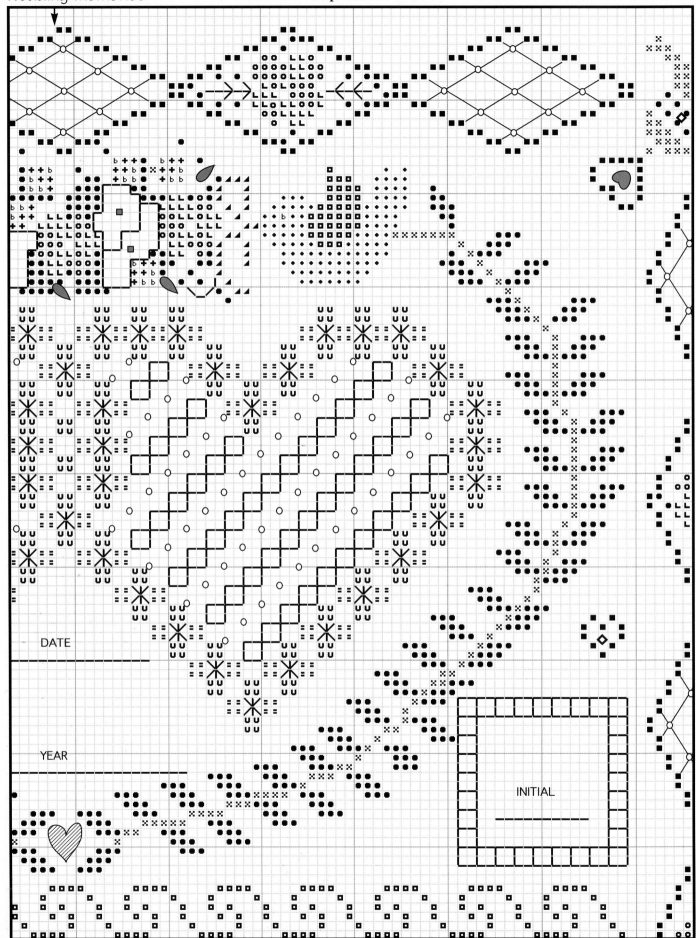

DATE

YEAR

INITIAL

_____

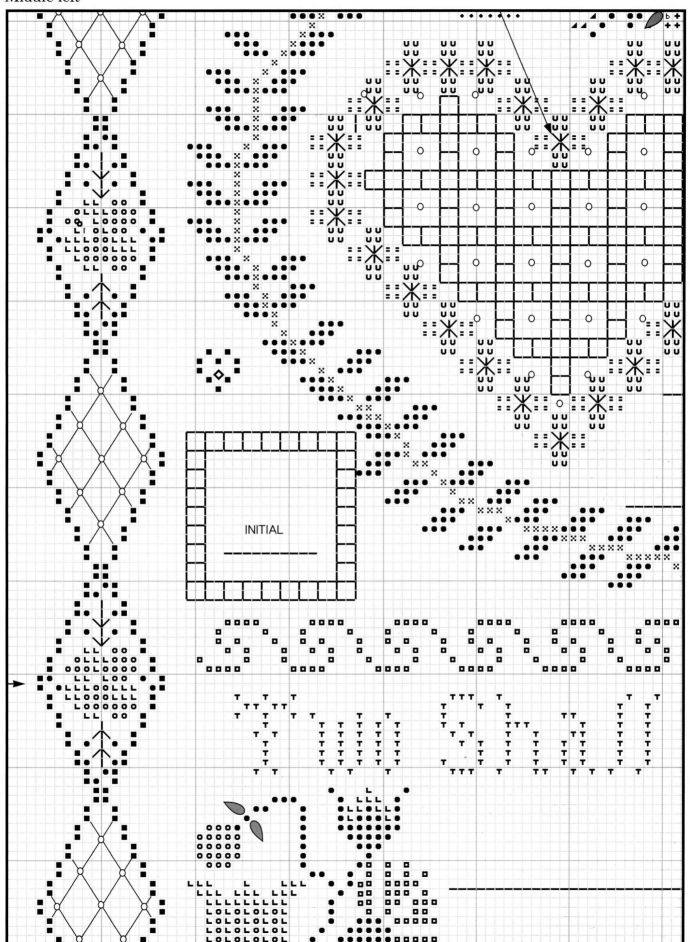

INITIAL

_____

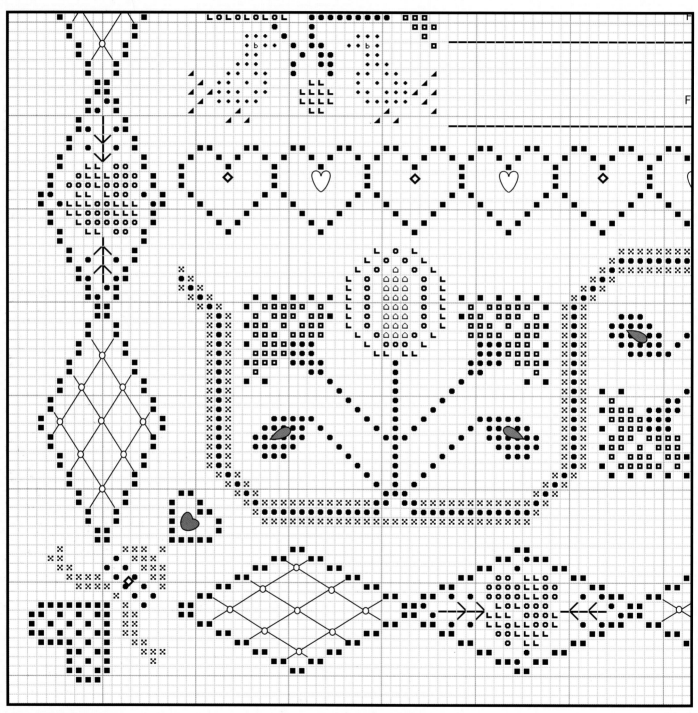

Bottom left

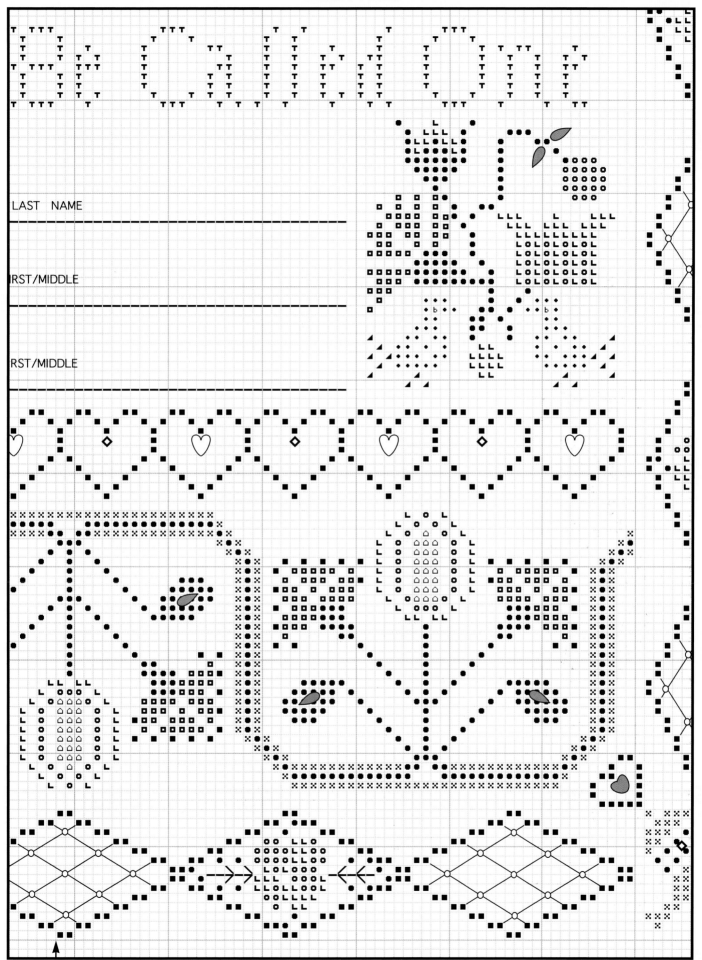

LAST NAME

IRST/MIDDLE

RST/MIDDLE

Top right

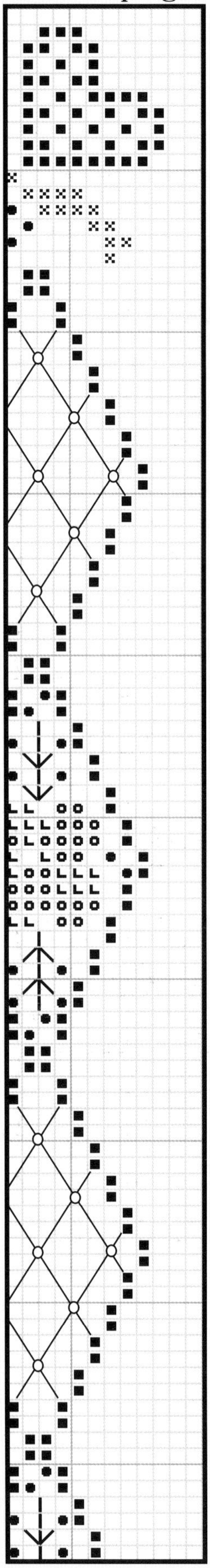

Middle right

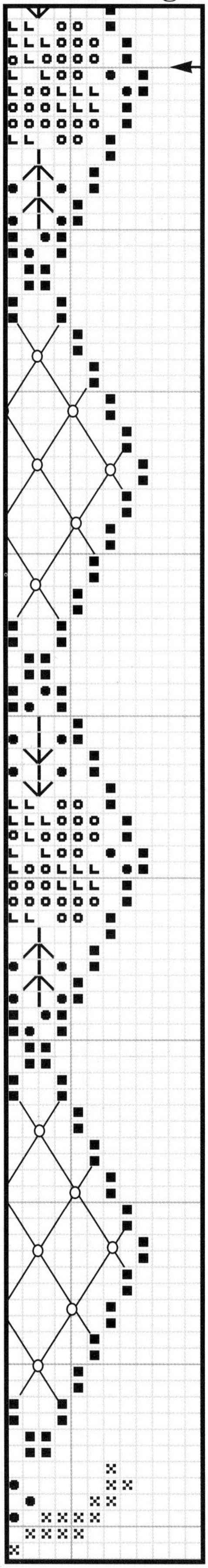

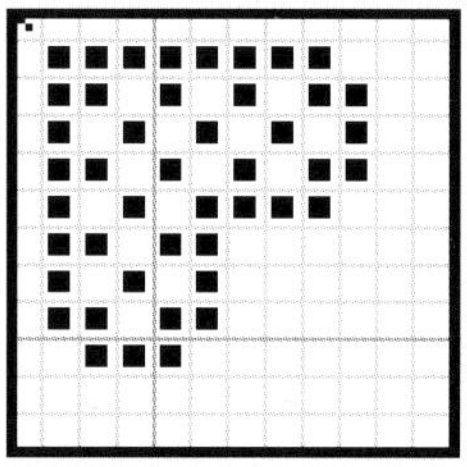

Bottom right

DMC Floss	XS	BS	ES	FSS	FS
Ecru			⋇	▭	⧉
223	⌂				
502		┐			
503	●				
739	T				
932		┐			
3752	•				

DMC Perle Cotton	KB
Ecru #8	⁝⁝
Ecru #8	UU

Kreinik	XS	#SPOOLS
002 #4Braid	◢	1

Mill Hill Beads	SYMBOL	ATT W/FLOSS	#PKGS
2006	ь	Ecru	1
2007	✚	Ecru	1
2016	⁙	502	2
2017	▣	932	2
3018	L	Ecru	2
3020	O	Ecru	2
3021	○ ■	Ecru	9
3021	▩	Ecru/bead loops(10)	

Mill Hill Treasures	SYMBOL	ATT W/BEAD/FLOSS	#PKGS
13031	◇	/Ecru	3
12143	●	/503	8
12086	♥	/Ecru	1
12092	♡	/Ecru	2
12214	♡	3021/Ecru	1

Large Alphabet

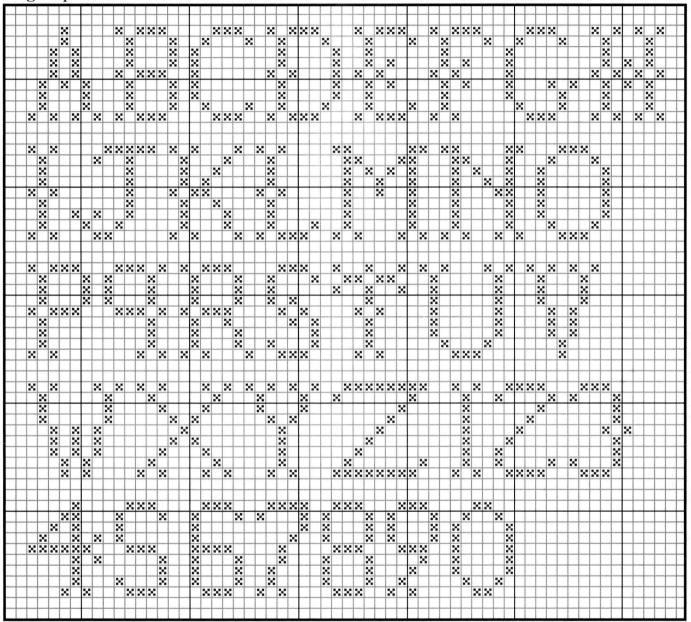

Anniversary Oval

Stitch Count: 88 x 68

Fabric: Linen, 25 count, driftwood

Special Instructions: At the dots around the yellow beads, using one strand of floss (822), pick up nine beads (3021). Return the needle in the first bead, go down in the same hole to form a loop. After entire project has been stitched and beaded, attach the glass treasures with the designated floss or beads.

Note: Refer to graph for treasure placement.

DMC Floss	XS	BS
561	G	
815		⌐

Kreinik	XS	#SPOOLS
002 #4 Braid	◢	1

Mill Hill Treasures

	SYMBOL	ATT W/BEAD/FLOSS	#PKGS
12143	◄	40161/822	4
12158	♨	40161/822	1
12155	♨	40161/822	3
12011	✹	168/822	2
12115	*see note	40161/822	1
12137	*see note	40161/822	1

Mill Hill Beads

	SYMBOL	ATT W/FLOSS	#PKGS
2005	✖	822	1
252	❂	822	1
3035	U	822	1
332	I	561	1
3028	◆	561	1
367	◙	822	1
3034	■	822	1
168	✚	822	1
3004	◤	822	1
2002	❍	822	1
2012	✦	822	1
553	＼	822	1
145	–	822	1
3021	◘	822/bead loops (9)	1
40161	UWT	822	1

Top left

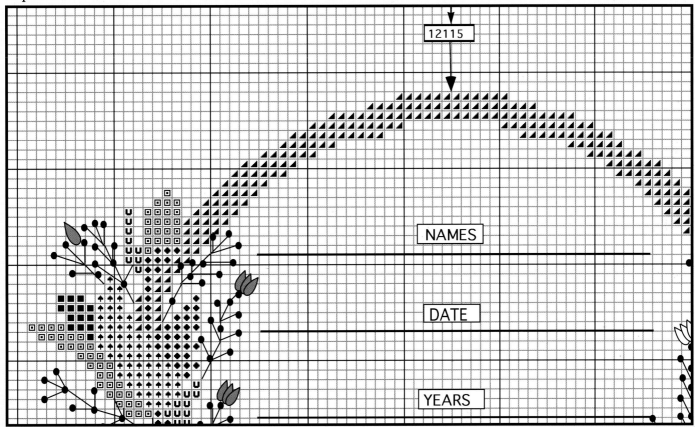

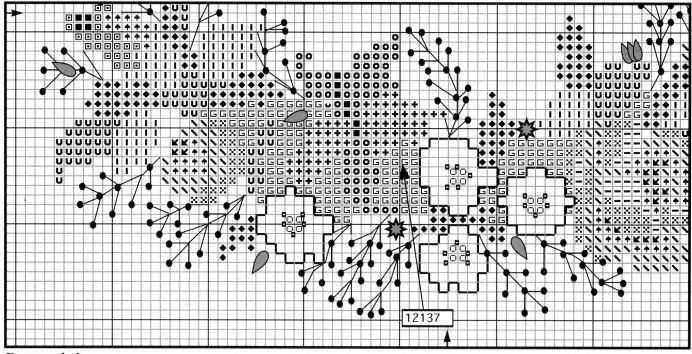

Bottom left

Top right

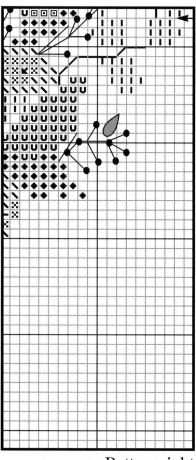

Bottom right

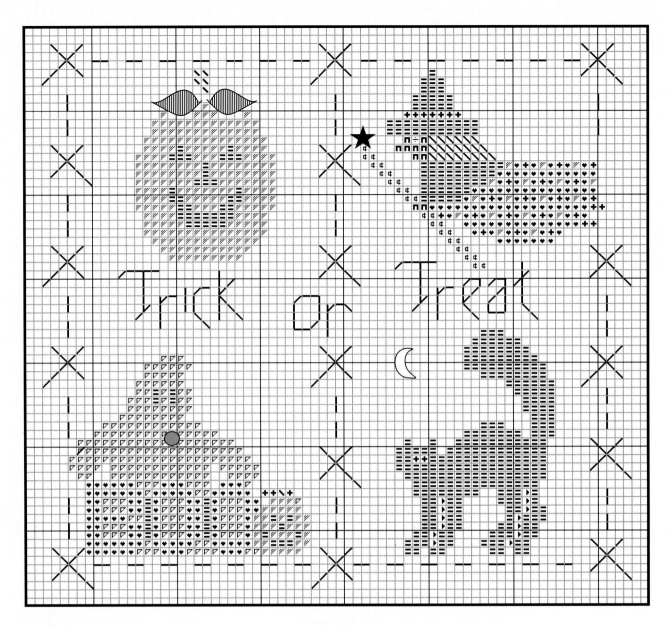

Halloween Night

Stitch Count: 69 x 65

Fabric: Aida, 14 count, natural

DMC Floss				
	LXS	BS	LS	RS
414 〉 646			\	
946 〉 918	X			-
918		⌐		

Mill Hill Beads			
	SYMBOL	ATT W/FLOSS	#PKGS
431	✚	3364	1
81	✤	310	1
148	⊓	761	1
150	▸	611	1
221	◣	611	1
358	÷	611	1
423	⧚	946	1
479	▽	White	1
556	⧺	611	1
2014	=	310	1

Mill Hill Treasures			
	SYMBOL	ATT W/FLOSS	#PKGS
12131	●	946	1
12185	☾	611	1
12171	★	310	1
12144	◈	3364	1

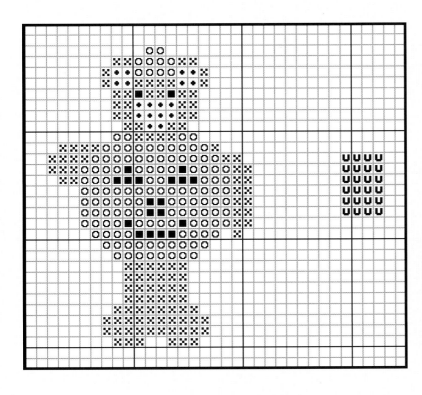

Trick-or-Treat Teddy

Stitch Count: 30 x 28

Fabric: Perforated paper, 14 count, ivory

Special Instructions: Using six strands of green floss from the front, go down through the center of the top of the bag and through the bear's paw. Tie a knot on the back to secure.

Mill Hill Beads			
	SYMBOL	ATT W/FLOSS	#PKGS
221	◆	Ecru	1
423	◑	Ecru	1
2014	■	Ecru	1
62023	✖	Ecru	1
62057	∪	Ecru	1

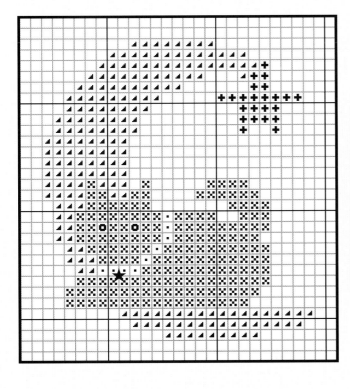

Moonbeam

Stitch Count: 25 x 28

Fabric: Perforated paper, 14 count, ivory

Mill Hill Beads			
	SYMBOL	ATT W/FLOSS	#PKGS
431	◘	Ecru	1
423	▪	Ecru	1
221	✚	Ecru	1
2014	✖	Ecru	1
62041	◢	Ecru	1
	★	Make a bead loop by picking up 2 (423), 1 (431), 2 (423) and go back down the same hole.	

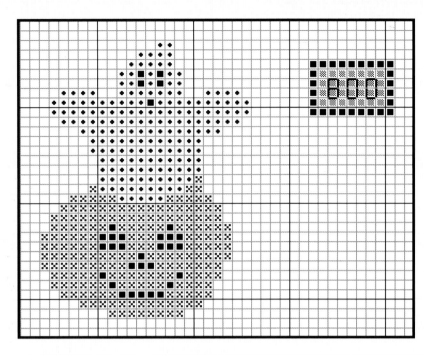

Pumpkin Boo

Stitch Count: 39 x 29

Fabric: Perforated paper, 14 count, brown

Special Instructions: Using six strands of black floss from the front, go down through the center of the ghost's hands. Come up and pick up the "Boo" and take running stitches across the top of the sign. Go down through the left hand and come up, leaving a "tail", creating the look that the ghost is carrying a sign.

DMC Floss	XS	BS
White	※	
310		⌐

Mill Hill Beads	SYMBOL	ATT W/FLOSS	#PKGS
423	✕	611	1
479	•	611	1
2014	■	611	1

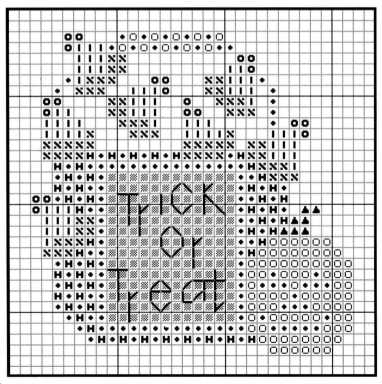

Trick-or-Treat Bag

Stitch Count: 30 x 30

Fabric: Perforated paper, 14 count, brown

DMC Floss	XS	BS
310	H	⌐
970	※	

Mill Hill Beads	SYMBOL	ATT W/FLOSS	#PKGS
332	♣	611	1
423	▫	611	1
2014	•	611	1
2058	◘	611	1
2059	I	611	1
2060	✕	611	1

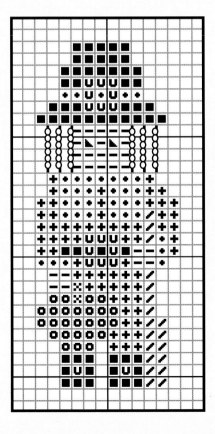

Pilgrim

Stitch Count: 12 x 29

Fabric: Perforated paper, 14 count, ivory

DMC Floss	
	XS
754	–
310	Bow

Mill Hill Beads			
	SYMBOL	ATT W/FLOSS	#PKGS
221	✎	Ecru	1
358	◣	Ecru	1
423	▣	Ecru	1
479	•	Ecru	1
2014	■	Ecru	1
62021	+	Ecru	1
62031	U	Ecru	1
62049	⋇	Ecru	1
42028	▮	Ecru/clusters(6)	1

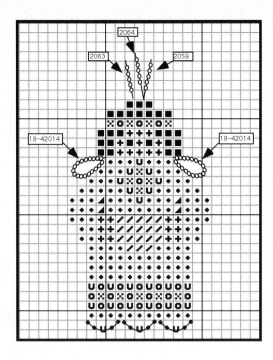

Indian Maiden

Stitch Count: 23 x 29

Fabric: Perforated paper, 14 count, ivory

Special Instructions: After attaching the beads for the hair braid, pick up two beads (2063) and attach beads over the top of each braid, at the base.

Note: Refer to graph for treasure placement.

DMC Floss	
	XS
758	+

Mill Hill Beads			
	SYMBOL	ATT W/FLOSS	#PKGS
2014	■	Ecru	1
2023	◢	Ecru	1
2059	○	Ecru	1
2059	*see note	Ecru/clusters(5)	
2063	U	Ecru	1
2063	*see note	Ecru/clusters(5)	
2064	✕	Ecru	1
2064	*see note	Ecru/clusters(5)	
62032	╱	Ecru	1
62057	✦	Ecru	1
42014	*see note	Ecru/bead loops(18)	1
	✦✦U✦✦	At each symbol pick up 2 (62057), 1 (2063), 2 (62057) and form loops as charted.	

Gobble Gobble

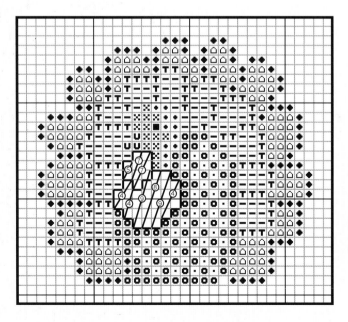

Stitch Count: 29 x 26

Fabric: Perforated paper, 14 count, brown

Note: Number in circle indicates amount of beads to use in each cluster.

DMC Floss	
	HX
355	▬
372	·
739	△

Mill Hill Beads			
	SYMBOL	ATT W/FLOSS	#PKGS
123	✦	739	1
128	U	355	1
330	T	355	1
2013	✕	739	1
2014	■	739	1
2021	◆	739	1
40123	*see note	739/clusters	1
62057	○	372	1
42013	*see note	739/clusters	1

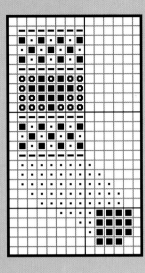

Christmas Socks

Stitch Count: 12 x 23 (each)

Fabric: Perforated paper, 14 count, brown

Special instructions: Using six strands of green floss from the back, come up at the top left-hand corner of the sock. Go down through the other sock at the same place. Tie floss in back to form a hanger.

DMC Floss	XS	Hanger
Ecru	·	
699	◘	

Mill Hill Beads			
	SYMBOL	ATT W/FLOSS	#PKGS
968	■	611	1
2020	▬	611	1

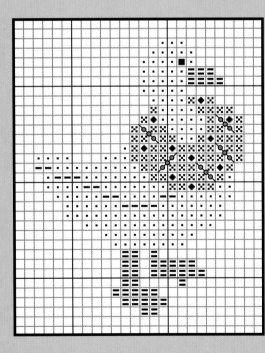

Christmas Goose

Stitch Count: 22 x 29

Fabric: Perforated paper, 14 count, brown

Mill Hill Beads			
	SYMBOL	ATT W/FLOSS	#PKGS
150	▬	611	1
167	✦	611	1
221	=	611	1
479	·	611	1
968	◘	611	1
2020	✖	611	1
2021	■	611	1
968	⟍	611/clusters(3)	

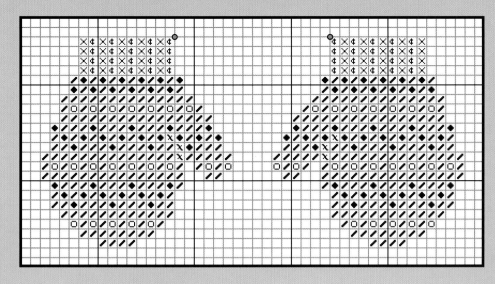

Mittens

Stitch Count: 20 x 22 (each)

Fabric: Perforated paper, 14 count, brown

Special Instructions: Using six strands of red floss from the back, come up at the top left- hand corner of the mitten, go down through the other mitten at the same spot. Tie floss in the back to form a hanger.

DMC Floss	XS	Hanger
304	✎	◯
902	✗	

Mill Hill Beads			
	SYMBOL	ATT W/FLOSS	#PKGS
968	✕	611	1
479	▢	611	1
367	✠	611	1
332	◆	611	1

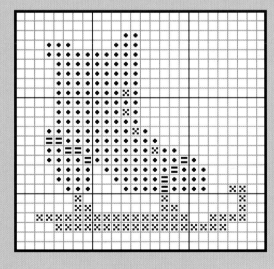

Skates

Stitch Count: 22 x 21 (each)

Fabric: Perforated paper, 14 count, white

Note: Using six strands of white floss from the back, come up at the top left- hand corner of the skate, go down through the other skate at the same spot. Tie floss in the back to form a hanger.

DMC Floss	Hanger
White	*see note

Mill Hill Beads			
	SYMBOL	ATT W/FLOSS	#PKGS
479	•	White	1
2017	=	White	1
2022	✖	White	1

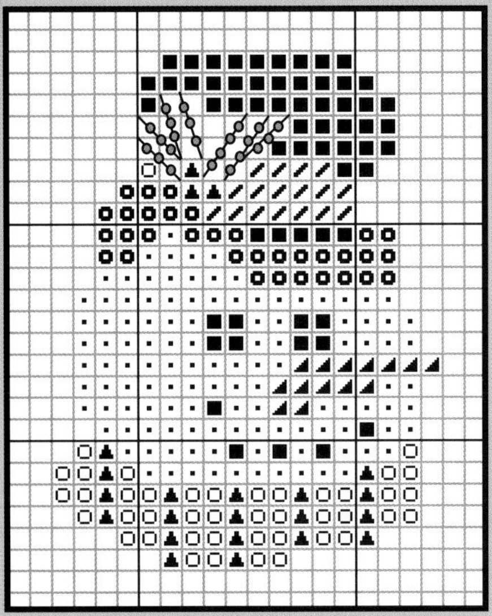

Frosty

Stitch Count: 18 x 24

Fabric: Perforated paper, 14 count, white

Mill Hill Beads			
	SYMBOL	ATT W/FLOSS	#PKGS
81	**O**	White	1
423	◢	White	1
479	▪	White	1
2013	▲	White	1
2014	■	White	1
2020	○	White	1
2020	-o-o-	White/clusters	
2021	/	White	1

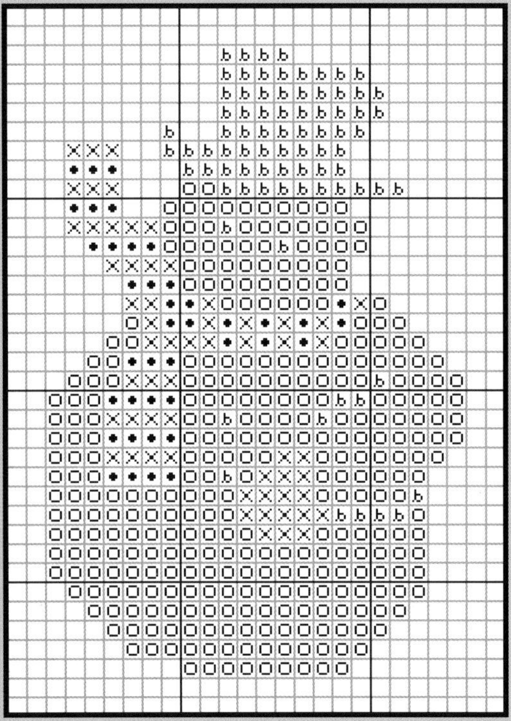

Snowman

Stitch Count: 23 x 33

Fabric: Perforated paper, 14 count, white

Mill Hill Beads			
	SYMBOL	ATT W/FLOSS	#PKGS
81	b	White	1
167	•	White	1
479	○	White	1
968	×	White	1

Candy Cane Penguin

Stitch Count: 20 x 30

Fabric: Perforated paper, 14 count, brown

Mill Hill Beads			
	SYMBOL	ATT W/FLOSS	#PKGS
167	–	611	1
479	/	611	1
557	L	611	1
2014	■	611	1
2021	T	611	1
2061	K	611	1
40479	-ooo-	611/clusters	1
62013	⊠	611	1

DMC Floss	
	XS
White	▪
304	**O**

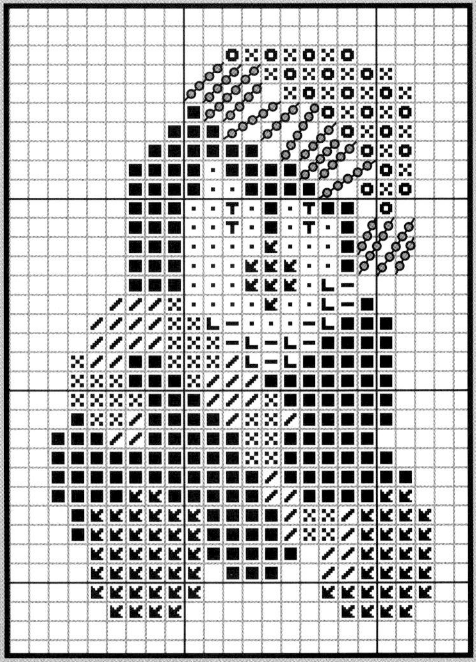

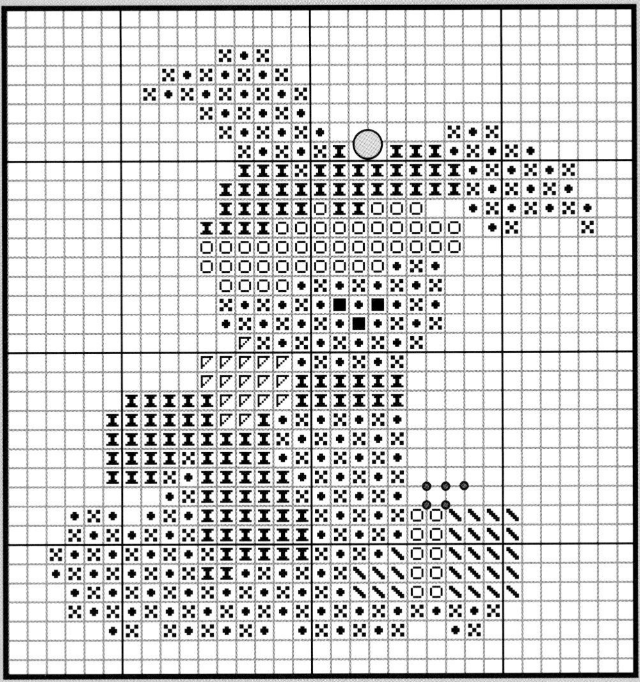

Jingle Bunny

Stitch count: 29 x 31

Fabric: Perforated paper, 14 count, white

DMC Floss	
	XS
White	⁙

Mill Hill Beads			
	SYMBOL	ATT W/FLOSS	#PKGS
60020	⧗	White	1
2013	o	White	1
557	◸	White	1
2020	⟍	White	1
62021	■	White	1
479	•	White	1
2013	⬬	White/bead loops (10)	1
MHBell	○	White	1

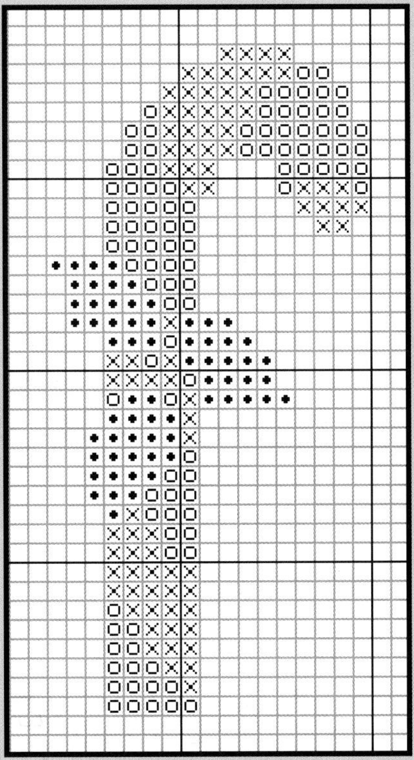

Candy Cane

Stitch Count: 17 x 35

Fabric: Perforated paper, 14 count, white

Mill Hill Beads			
	SYMBOL	ATT W/FLOSS	#PKGS
332	•	White	1
479	×	White	1
968	o	White	1

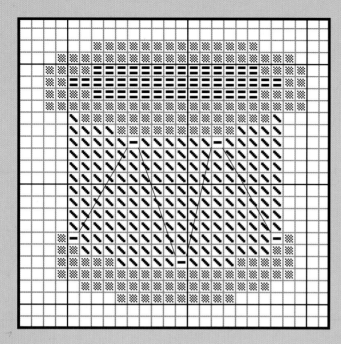

Toy Drum

Stitch Count: 22 x 22

Fabric: Perforated paper, 14 count, brown

DMC Floss		
	XS	LS
304	\	
310		/

Mill Hill Beads			
	SYMBOL	ATT W/FLOSS	#PKGS
557	–	611	1
123	=	611	1
20	※	611	1

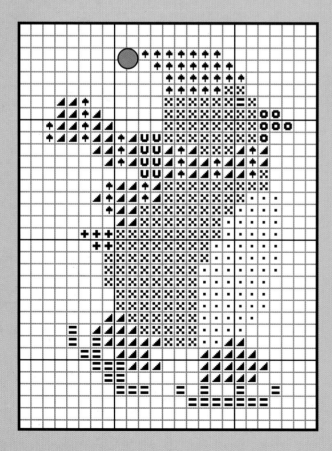

Skating Penguin

Stitch Count: 21 x 30

Fabric: Perforated paper, 14 count, white

Mill Hill Beads			
	SYMBOL	ATT W/FLOSS	#PKGS
2013	◢	White	1
2014	✖	White	1
128	✿	White	1
81	✛	White	1
479	·	White	1
2022	=	White	1
367	U	White	1
2020	✦	White	1
MHBell	●	White	1

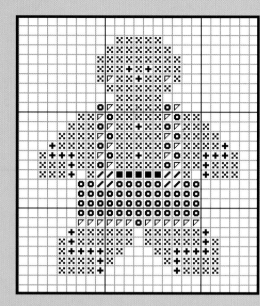

Gingerbread Boy

Stitch Count: 21 x 25

Fabric: Perforated paper, 14 count, ivory

DMC Floss	
890	Bow

Mill Hill Beads			
	SYMBOL	ATT W/FLOSS	#PKGS
2011	✎	Ecru	1
2014	■	Ecru	1
2020	✿	Ecru	1
2023	✕	Ecru	1
2058	✛	Ecru	1
2063	▽	Ecru	1

Gingerbread House

Stitch Count: 25 x 27

Fabric: Perforated paper, 14 count, brown

Mill Hill Beads			
	SYMBOL	ATT W/FLOSS	#PKGS
167	•	611	1
968	▢	611	1
128	Y	611	1
479	W	611	1

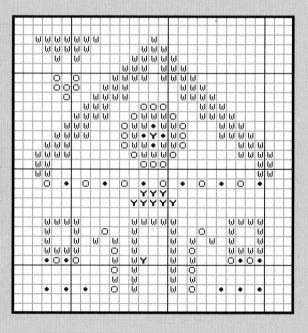

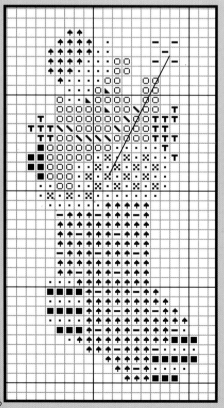

Stocking Teddy

Stitch Count: 18 x 37

Fabric: Perforated paper, 14 count, white

Krienik		
	LS	#SPOOLS
002 #4 Braid	╲	1

DMC Floss	
	XS
White	✕

Mill Hill Beads			
	SYMBOL	ATT W/FLOSS	#PKGS
167	T	White	1
221	╲	White	1
479	•	White	1
557	—	White	1
2013	✛	White	1
2014	◣	White	1
2023	▢	White	1
62020	■	White	1

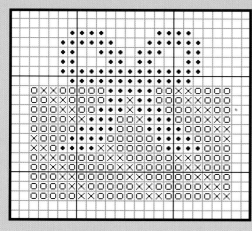

Gift Package

Stitch Count: 21 x 18

Fabric: Perforated paper, 14 count, white

Mill Hill Beads			
	SYMBOL	ATT W/FLOSS	#PKGS
479	✕	White	1
332	•	White	1
968	▢	White	1

O red.
X white
❀ green

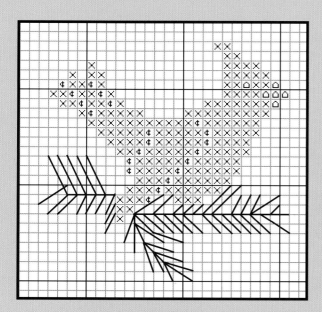

Cardinal

Stitch Count: 26 x 25

Fabric: Perforated paper, 14 count, brown

DMC Floss	
	LS
3818	╱

Mill Hill Beads			
	SYMBOL	ATT W/FLOSS	#PKGS
968	✕	611	1
2014	▢	611	1
367	¢	611	1

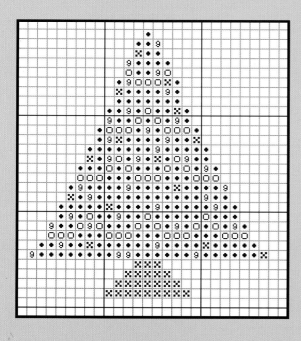

Christmas Tree

Stitch Count: 25 x 28

Fabric: Perforated paper, 14 count, brown

Mill Hill Beads			
	SYMBOL	ATT W/FLOSS	#PKGS
167	9	611	1
332	•	611	1
557	✖	611	1
968	▢	611	1

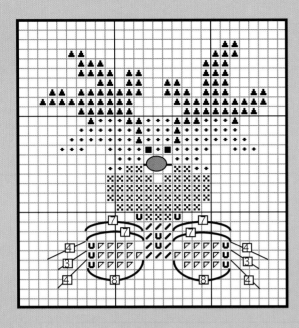

Rudy

Stitch Count: 24 x 26

Fabric: Perforated paper, 14 count, brown

Note: Number in square indicates amount of beads to use in each cluster. Clusters of seven and eight use beads (62020). Clusters of three and four use beads (2013).

Mill Hill Beads			
	SYMBOL	ATT W/FLOSS	#PKGS
221	♣	Ecru	1
2011	╱	Ecru	1
2013	◹	Ecru	1
2013	*see note	Ecru/clusters	
5025	⬭	Ecru	1
42014	■	Ecru	1
62023	✦	Ecru	1
62020	U	Ecru	1
62020	*see note	Ecru/clusters	
62057	✕	Ecru	1

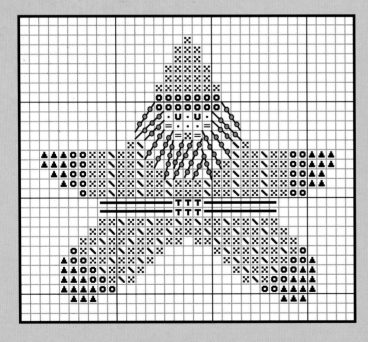

Star Santa

Stitch Count: 31 x 28

Fabric: Perforated paper, 14 count, white

Mill Hill Beads			
	SYMBOL	ATT W/FLOSS	#PKGS
145	·	White	1
358	U	White	1
479	⊙	White	1
479	-◍◍◍-	White/clusters	
2005	=	White	1
2013	✕	White	1
2020	╲	White	1
62014	♣	White	1
72011	т т т	White	1
92014	▬▬	White	1

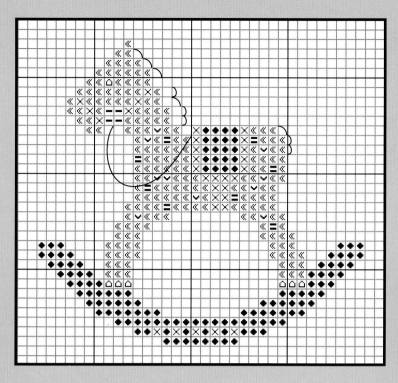

Rocking Horse

Stitch Count: 34 x 32

Fabric: Perforated paper, 14 count, brown

Special Instructions: Cut out the ornament, following the marked line at the area of the mane. Thread the needle with six strands of grey floss.

The unmarked spaces on the mane are where these stitches are to be worked. Go down in the paper from the front, leaving a loop on the back. Come up, crossing one space, then go back through the loop with threaded needle. Pull the loose end through the loop also and pull the ends tight. Trim to ⅜". Repeat.

There are eight fringe stitches for the mane and three fringe stitches for the tail. Trim tail to about 1¼". Attach a red floss lead as shown on graph.

DMC Floss	
414	Mane
304	Rein

Mill Hill Beads			
	SYMBOL	ATT W/FLOSS	#PKGS
968	×	611	1
2014	⌂	611	1
557	−	611	1
332	◆	611	1
150	«	611	1
123	=	611	1
81	⌄	611	1

Stocking

Stitch Count: 25 x 39

Fabric: Perforated paper, 14 count, brown

DMC Floss	
	XS
225	F
304	×
224	✦

Mill Hill Beads			
	SYMBOL	ATT W/FLOSS	#PKGS
332	•	611	1
479	▢	611	1
128	Y	611	1
358	♭	611	1
367	∪	611	1
968	r	611	1
167	9	611	1
557	╱	611	1

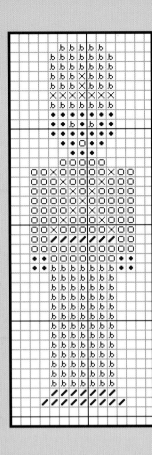

Toy Soldier

Stitch Count: 11 x 38

Fabric: Perforated paper, 14 count, brown

Mill Hill Beads			
	SYMBOL	ATT W/FLOSS	#PKGS
20	♭	611	1
81	◢	611	1
145	✦	611	1
557	✕	611	1
968	◻	611	1

Feather Tree

Stitch Count: 25 x 33

Fabric: Perforated paper, 14 count, white

Mill Hill Beads			
	SYMBOL	ATT W/FLOSS	#PKGS
2020	✕	White	1
62013	▪	White	1
72020	╲	White	1

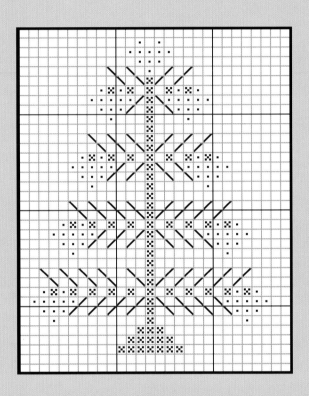

Noel Heart

Stitch Count: 27 x 23

Fabric: Perforated paper, 14 count, white

DMC Floss	
	LS
699	╲

Mill Hill Beads			
	SYMBOL	ATT W/FLOSS	#PKGS
968	◢	White	1
2020	✕	White	1

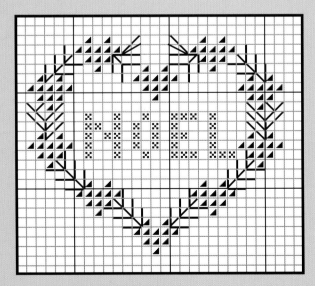

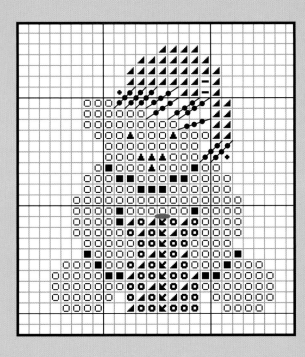

Santa Teddy

Stitch Count: 21 x 25

Fabric: Perforated paper, 14 count, white

Krienik		
	Bow	#SPOOLS
002HL #4 Braid	⬭	1

Mill Hill Beads			
	SYMBOL	ATT W/FLOSS	#PKGS
968	◢	White	1
479	✚	White	1
2020	◘	White	1
2014	▲	White	1
2023	◻	White	1
330	■	White	1
367	▬	White	1
557	◤	White	1
479	╱	White/clusters(3)	1

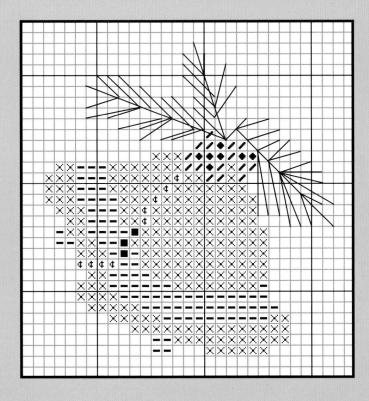

Bells

Stitch Count: 27 x 29

Fabric: Perforated paper, 14 count, brown

DMC Floss	
	LS
3818	╱

Mill Hill Beads			
	SYMBOL	ATT W/FLOSS	#PKGS
968	✕	611	1
557	▬	611	1
367	₵	611	1
2012	╱	611	1
332	♣	611	1
221	■	611	1

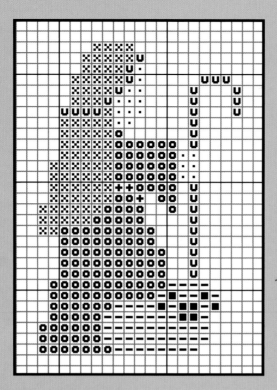

Shepherd

Stitch Count: 19 x 29

Fabric: Perforated paper, 14 count, white

Mill Hill Beads			
	SYMBOL	ATT W/FLOSS	#PKGS
358	✚	White	1
367	✕	White	1
221	U	White	1
2015	▣	White	1
145	·	White	1
81	■	White	1
479	▬	White	1

Christmas Sampler

Photo and graph on pages 115–119.

Stitch Count: 103 x 205

Fabric: Linen, 28 count, natural

Mill Hill Treasures			
	SYMBOL	ATT W/BEAD/FLOSS	#PKGS
13022	⬤	/815	6
13034	◆	/815	9
12217	◀	/815	3
12056	▸◂	/815	3
12197	◣	/890	6
12077	♥	557/815	3
13027	◆	/642	6
12036	✳	557/642	5
13026	◇	/890	12
12168	★	/815	6
12188	★	62032/815	10
12207	♡	/815	4

DMC Floss	
	XS
815	I
890	✕

Mill Hill Beads			
	SYMBOL	ATT W/FLOSS	#PKGS
557	✚	642	2
2020	◢	890	3
62032	■	815	2

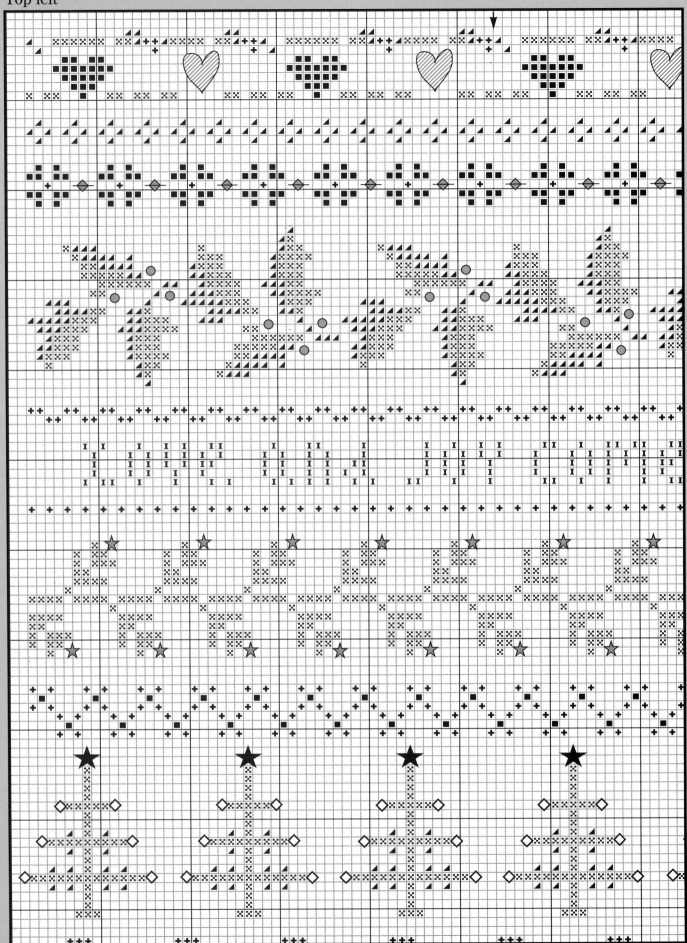

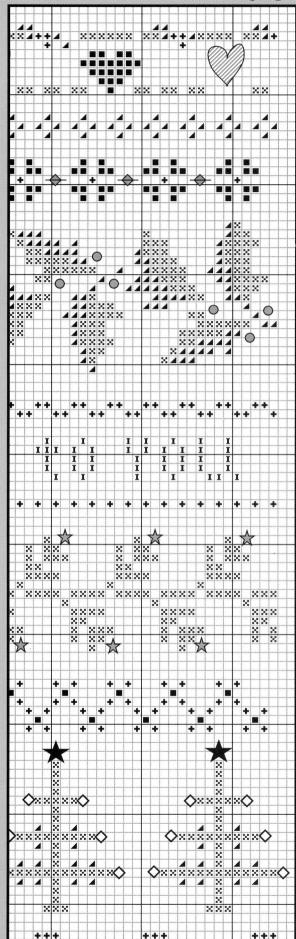

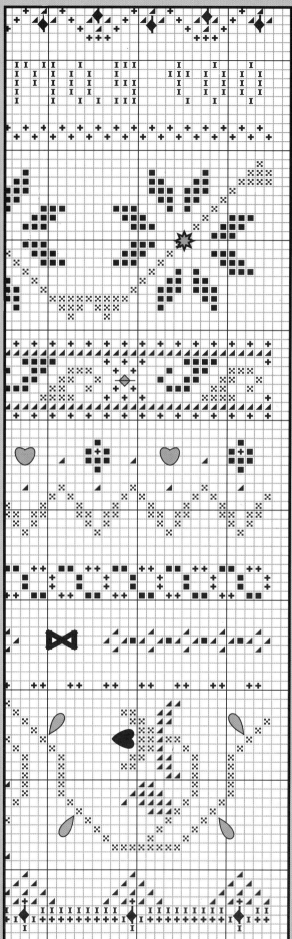

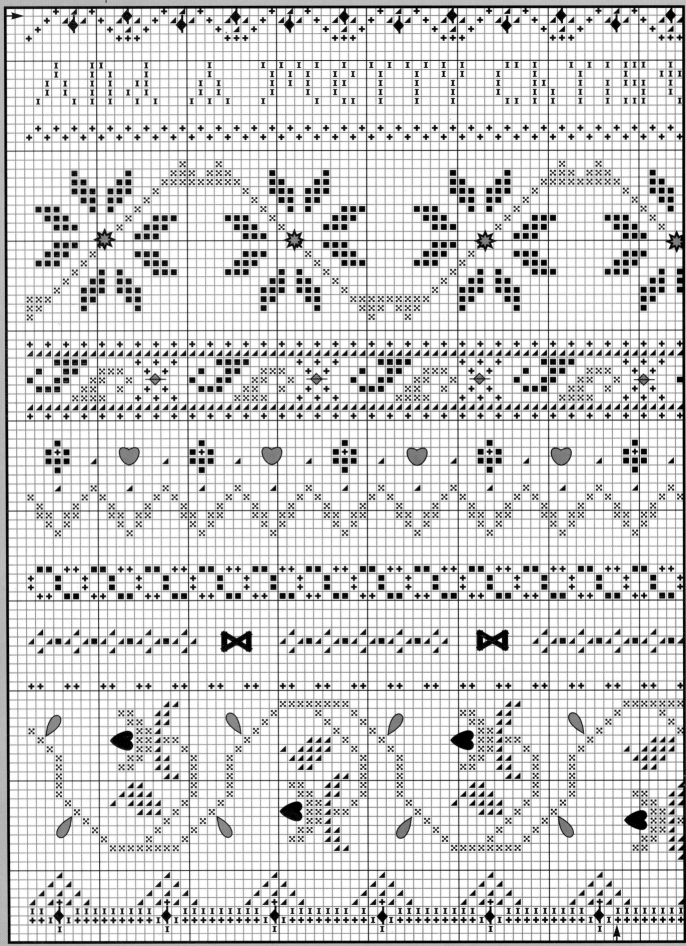

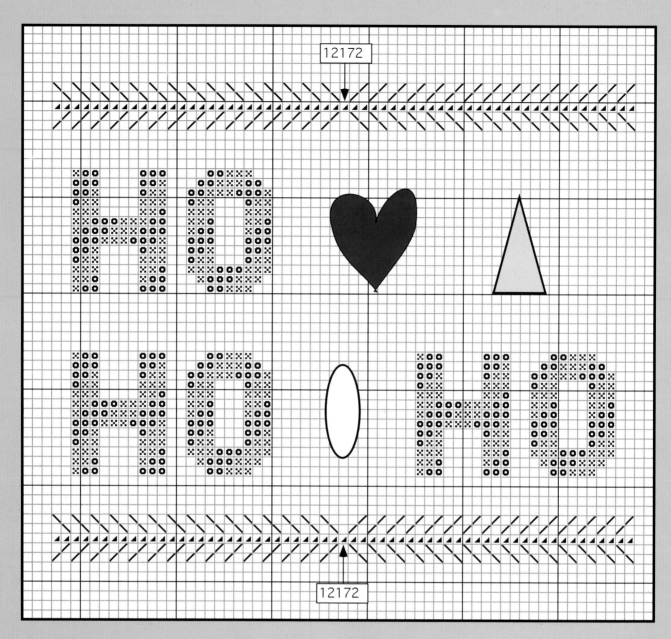

Ho Ho Ho

Stitch Count: 60 x 50

Fabric: Aida, 14 count, natural

Note: Refer to graph for treasure placement.

DMC Floss		
	XS	LS
890	◢	╲

Mill Hill Beads			
	SYMBOL	ATT W/FLOSS	#PKGS
968	◖	611	1
479	✖	611	1

Mill Hill Treasures			
	SYMBOL	ATT W/BEAD/FLOSS	#PKGS
12172	*see note	/816	2
12215	♥	/816	1
12112	○	479/White	1
12179	Δ	332/890	1

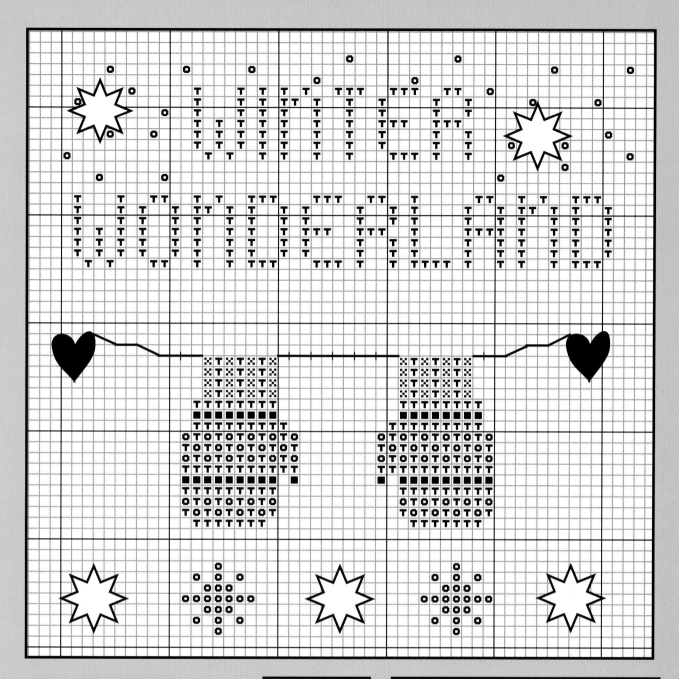

Winter Wonderland

Stitch Count: 51 x 54

Fabric: Aida, 14 count, natural

DMC Floss		
	XS	BS
304	T	
816	✖	⌐

Mill Hill Beads			
	SYMBOL	ATT W/FLOSS	#PKGS
2020	■	611	1
123	✿	611	1

Mill Hill Treasures			
	SYMBOL	ATT W/FLOSS	#PKGS
12207	♥	816	2
15001	☆	611	2

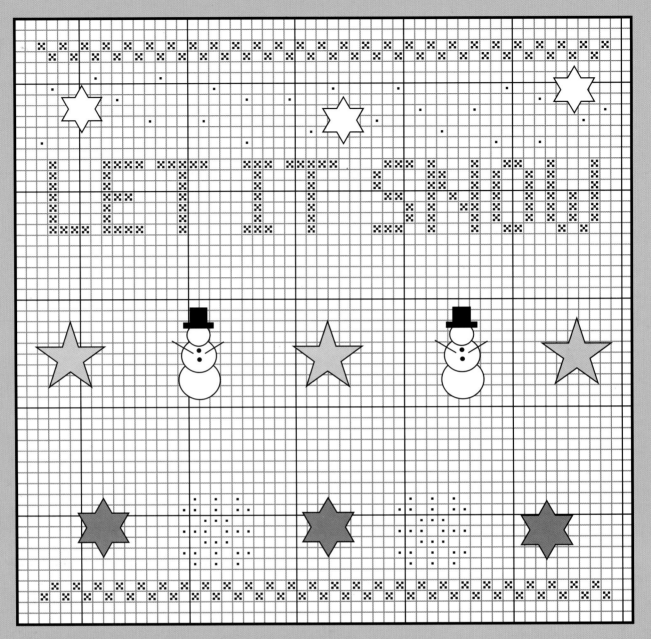

Let It Snow

Stitch Count: 53 x 52

Fabric: Aida, 14 count, natural

DMC Floss	
	XS
498	✗

Mill Hill Beads			
	SYMBOL	ATT W/FLOSS	#PKGS
123	▪	611	1

Mill Hill Treasures			
	SYMBOL	ATT W/BEAD/FLOSS	#PKGS
12162	★	/611	3
12161	☆	/611	3
12175	★	479/611	3
12060	☃	/611	1

Peace Mantel Cloth

Stitch Count: 173 x 37

Fabric: Banding,
24 count, burgundy
with gold edging

Kreinik		
	XS	**#SPOOLS**
002 #4 Braid	✖	3

Mill Hill Beads			
	SYMBOL	**ATT W/FLOSS**	**#PKGS**
3035	■	500	6

Top left

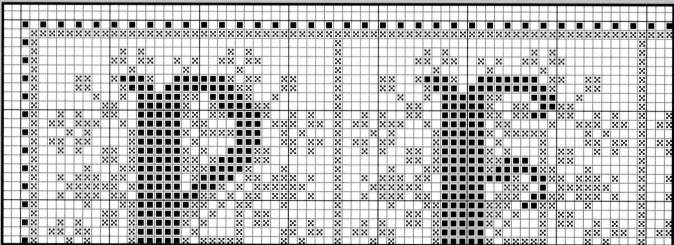

Top center

Bottom left

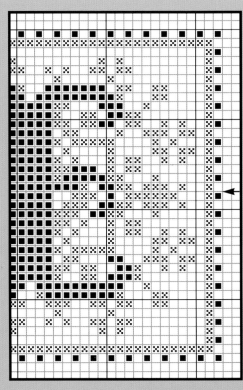

Bottom right

Metric Conversion Chart

mm-millimetres cm-centimetres
inches to millimetres and centimetres

inches	mm	cm	inches	cm	inches	cm
⅛	3	0.3	9	22.9	30	76.2
¼	6	0.6	10	25.4	31	78.7
⅜	10	1.0	11	27.9	32	81.3
½	13	1.3	12	30.5	33	83.8
⅝	16	1.6	13	33.0	34	86.4
¾	19	1.9	14	35.6	35	88.9
⅞	22	2.2	15	38.1	36	91.4
1	25	2.5	16	40.6	37	94.0
1¼	32	3.2	17	43.2	38	96.5
1½	38	3.8	18	45.7	39	99.1
1¾	44	4.4	19	48.3	40	101.6
2	51	5.1	20	50.8	41	104.1
2½	64	6.4	21	53.3	42	106.7
3	76	7.6	22	55.9	43	109.2
3½	89	8.9	23	58.4	44	111.8
4	102	10.2	24	61.0	45	114.3
4½	114	11.4	25	63.5	46	116.8
5	127	12.7	26	66.0	47	119.4
6	152	15.2	27	68.6	48	121.9
7	178	17.8	28	71.1	49	124.5
8	203	20.3	29	73.7	50	127.0

yards to metres

yards	metres	yards	metres	yards	metres	yards	metres	yards	metres
⅛	0.11	2⅛	1.94	4⅛	3.77	6⅛	5.60	8⅛	7.43
¼	0.23	2¼	2.06	4¼	3.89	6¼	5.72	8¼	7.54
⅜	0.34	2⅜	2.17	4⅜	4.00	6⅜	5.83	8⅜	7.66
½	0.46	2½	2.29	4½	4.11	6½	5.94	8½	7.77
⅝	0.57	2⅝	2.40	4⅝	4.23	6⅝	6.06	8⅝	7.89
¾	0.69	2¾	2.51	4¾	4.34	6¾	6.17	8¾	8.00
⅞	0.80	2⅞	2.63	4⅞	4.46	6⅞	6.29	8⅞	8.12
1	0.91	3	2.74	5	4.57	7	6.40	9	8.23
1⅛	1.03	3⅛	2.86	5⅛	4.69	7⅛	6.52	9⅛	8.34
1¼	1.14	3¼	2.97	5¼	4.80	7¼	6.63	9¼	8.46
1⅜	1.26	3⅜	3.09	5⅜	4.91	7⅜	6.74	9⅜	8.57
1½	1.37	3½	3.20	5½	5.03	7½	6.86	9½	8.69
1⅝	1.49	3⅝	3.31	5⅝	5.14	7⅝	6.97	9⅝	8.80
1¾	1.60	3¾	3.43	5¾	5.26	7¾	7.09	9¾	8.92
1⅞	1.71	3⅞	3.54	5⅞	5.37	7⅞	7.20	9⅞	9.03
2	1.83	4	3.66	6	5.49	8	7.32	10	9.14

Index